Successful
Self-Publishing

Successful Self-Publishing
MAKING AND SELLING YOUR OWN BOOK

SHERRYL CLARK

© 1997 Sherryl Clark

This book is copyright. Apart from any fair dealing for the purpose of study, research, criticism, review, or as otherwise permitted under the Copyright Act, no part may be reproduced by any process without written permission. Inquiries should be made to the publisher.

First edition
10 9 8 7 6 5 4 3 2 1

Typeset by
DOCUPRO, Sydney

Printed & bound by
Southwood Press Pty Ltd
80–92 Chapel St, Marrickville, NSW

For the publisher
Hale & Iremonger Pty Limited
PO Box 205, Alexandria 2015

*National Library of Australia
Cataloguing-in-Publication*

Clark, Sherryl.
    Successful self-publishing: making and selling your own book.

    Bibliography.
    ISBN 0 86806 626 5.

    1. Self-publishing—Australia. I. Title.

070.5930994

Contents

	Acknowledgements	vi
	Introduction	ix
1	Why are you doing it?	1
2	The pros and cons of self-publishing	8
3	Making initial decisions — The end before the beginning	13
4	Writing and editing	21
5	Some important technicalities	29
6	Typesetting and proofreading	40
7	Saving money and keeping quality	47
8	The look of the book	53
9	Limitations and problems	66
10	What else apart from the text?	70
11	The cover	78
12	Methods of printing	83
13	Getting quotes	89
14	Costing your book	94
15	Preparation and printing	101
16	Pre-publicity and the launch	106
17	Distribution and marketing	111
18	Finally . . .	128
	Appendix 1: Hand binding	131
	Appendix 2: Starting and publishing a magazine	134
	Appendix 3: Bibliography	136
	Glossary	139
	Index	149

Acknowledgements

Many thanks to the following for their advice, ideas, information, feedback and support: Adrienne Mazer Swinton, Margaret Campbell, Lorraine Neate, Tracey Rolfe, Lissa Mitchell, Sylvia Kirwan, Helen North, Cliff Smyth, Doris Leadbetter, Kristin Henry, Pariah Press Co-operative, the self-publishing and marketing students and staff at Blackwood Street Neighbourhood House, Rosemary Wildblood (Creative New Zealand), Hazel Edwards, Keith Hawkins and staff (Printing Services Unit, Western Melbourne Institute of TAFE), Paul Holmes and staff (Quickset Press, Yarraville), the Victorian Writers' Centre, and especially Brian McCabe.

The New Zealand references were kindly supplied by Daphne Brasell Associates, Press and Publishing Services, Wellington, New Zealand.

For Adrienne

Introduction

How do we define 'successful' self-publishing? In the past, success has been judged in terms of competing with the commercial publishers, with print runs in the thousands, and coming out the other end without losing your shirt. Many people decided self-publishing was out of their reach because they simply didn't have the money, the expertise or the marketing abilities to compete. The necessity of using offset presses, plates and all the costs and paraphernalia that went with those processes also made it prohibitive for many.

Things have changed. New technologies and easier access to them means anyone can produce a book with their home computer and a decent photocopier. But the other change, one of attitude, is a bit slow in catching up. Success is still defined by printing thousands of copies and winning in the commercial arena, when the most exciting aspect of self-publishing now is its ability to excel in the niche areas where the big publishers can no longer afford to compete.

If our hundreds of practising poets stopped printing up their poems, if our family history enthusiasts stopped creating books out of their passions, if all the people with special skills and knowledge stopped finding ways of writing them down and publishing for everyone else, we would be immeasurably worse off. If all of those self-publishers were expected to sell in the thousands to prove their books were worthwhile, who would bother?

Successful Self-Publishing

Successful self-publishing is simply about selling the books you produce, whether that be 50, 300 or 2000. Or, if you're not interested in selling, giving them away to your appreciative audience. Boxes of books going mouldy in your garage or utilised for the next ten years as makeshift furniture is not publishing successfully.

This book is designed to help you be successful on your own terms. It aims to be practical, to help you avoid the pitfalls and mistakes where possible, and to guide you in a venture which is both enjoyable and achievable. Not one which causes you to lose sleep or, at the very worst, your house.

Successful Self-Publishing gives you the information necessary to make practical decisions and formulate a publishing and marketing plan. You can choose to do everything yourself, or employ professionals as required. I have worked with over eighty self-publishers in the past five years and seen more than a hundred publications of every shape, size and subject launched to genuine acclaim. You can do it too.

Sherryl Clark

1 Why are you doing it?

There are many reasons for self-publishing your own book, and this is really the first question you need to ask yourself. In all aspects of planning your book you must be realistic and honest, but especially so in these early stages. This is where the answers to your questions relate to the end of the process — whether you will be selling or not. If you are fooling yourself about why you are self-publishing, you will make wrong decisions all the way down the line.

Usually your reasons involve either your head, your heart or your wallet, or perhaps a combination. Just because you have the desire to publish a collection of your poetry, doesn't mean you can't make at least a small profit.

A record of your achievement

Many people write for years and simply want a quality publication which reflects their work and achievement. This is particularly so in areas such as poetry or autobiography where the chances of commercial publication are very low. This is not vanity publishing — vanity publishing these days refers to fancy printer/publishers who charge you lots of money to produce hundreds of copies of your book in a fancy binding, pretending they are 'real' publishers with distribution and selling outlets. You pay for the printing but have little control over your books;

it's better to do it all yourself and at a much cheaper price. And they publish absolutely anything, no matter how awful, which is why they have a bad reputation.

If your aim is to publish writing you are proud of, go right ahead. But answer the questions on how many are likely to buy your book very honestly. If you don't see yourself as a crackerjack salesperson, remember that there can be as much enjoyment in producing a book to give as a gift as there is in producing one to sell.

An ever-growing area of self-published books is the autobiography/ biography/family history field. I know of one woman who spent twenty years researching her family history and the resulting book was a wonderful reward for all her work. Writers of family histories have a ready audience and may also be able to get financial assistance from their relatives for printing costs. It is also the kind of material which should be published—the histories of ordinary lives which are often overlooked.

You as a writer

The next step up from that achievement is the belief that you have a commercially viable book, whether it's a novel, a collection of stories, an autobiography or whatever, but you can't find a commercial publisher who will take it. Most commercial first novels have a print run of around 2,000 to 4,000 with efficient marketing and distribution to back them up. If you want to self-publish a book that will be competitive in this market, you must be prepared to undertake the business side which comes with that, as well as the considerable financial outlay.

You need to think about editing, making it look like a 'real' book, how you can market and distribute it, and be sensible about your print run. Think in terms of hundreds, not thousands, initially, unless you have plenty of time and energy to market and distribute. In densely populated areas in England and the U.S.A., self-publishers can distribute and sell their books in much larger numbers than here. In Australia we are hampered by our geography, so the job of physically getting our books in front of our customers is difficult and costly.

Why are you doing it?

Some writers believe that if they self-publish first, this will attract the attention of a commercial publisher who will take them on and republish. It does happen: James Douglas printed 5000 copies of his thriller novel, *The Clearing Place*, and used a distributor as well as his own efforts to sell most of the copies. His aim was to have his next novel published commercially and Penguin Books offered him a contract. However he is the exception, not the rule, and the genre in which he was writing is more commercially viable than many others.

Many other writers just believe that what they have written should be in print — they want to communicate with readers and make a contribution to literature. Because commercial publishers need to make a profit, they will often turn down manuscripts because they aren't a safe enough 'bet' in the marketplace. The trouble is, this means we end up with bookshops full of mainstream literature which, however attractively it's packaged, doesn't contribute much in the way of new ideas and innovative writing. Self-publishing can play a very important role in introducing variety, new concepts and new, sometimes controversial, viewpoints. If you are passionate about your book, if you believe it should be published, you will be prepared to commit yourself to the whole process. Just don't bankrupt yourself in the process.

You have something to say

You may have a viewpoint you want to express, on a topic which you feel needs more debate or a more informed interpretation. It could be on politics, religion, health, history — the list is endless.

You may not need a book. A booklet or pamphlet-style publication may be more effective. You need to decide how much you want to say and the most effective way of presenting your material. Keep in mind also that people may not want to pay to hear what you are saying — you might be better off giving your publication away, especially if it is small and doesn't cost you much. For you, having a voice may be more important than making money.

A student of mine, Neil Simpson, self-published *Macedonia:*

Its Disputed History. He spent five years researching his book, including two visits to Macedonia, and believed that much of what had been said or reported was wrong or misinterpreted. He wanted to present a well-informed analysis, one that was both readable and useful, and achieved this after many hours wrestling with his laptop during final editing and proofreading (the price of accuracy).

Another woman, whose son had suffered terribly from undiagnosed food allergies, wanted to publish a book which alerted medical practitioners as well as parents to the dangers of food allergies. She did not manage to achieve her goal, mainly due to lack of time for more in-depth research, but other books have since become available on the subject and she continues to campaign herself.

Publishing with/for others

There are often instances where a writer who is asked to compile a local or particular history, perhaps of an area or an organisation or company, is also given the task of publishing the work. While the printing may be paid for by the organisation, all other aspects are the responsibility of the author. You need to be very clear about what kind of book is required, how much money is available and how it will be sold. It's no fun completing and printing five years of work if the boxes of books languish in the storeroom, or the local historical society has a 'falling out' and no-one is interested in the book any more.

Clarify details such as copyright and payments and get it all in writing. You may choose, for example, to take a third of the copies to sell yourself and keep the proceeds, rather than keep track of royalties. In this case you would have to negotiate who sells where so there's no treading on toes. If the book goes out of print, all rights should revert to you.

You may also find a very small publisher with whom you can form a partnership. You provide the money and they take care of the printing and distribution, with agreed repayments and profit sharing. Again, negotiate and get it all in writing.

Why are you doing it?

Selling knowledge

There are lots of people in this world with particular skills and knowledge. Putting this into a book can be an excellent publishing venture. Some examples include old or special recipes, fishing hints, craft techniques, advice on herbs — anything which either hasn't been previously covered or not covered well. Investigate whether any other books have been published on your area of expertise and check them out — you don't want to be re-inventing the wheel.

If a 'how-to' book is what you want to do, you will need to pay close attention to your illustrations. In some areas, the illustrations or diagrams are the most important part. You may have to pay someone to draw them for you if you can't do a quality job yourself. You cannot use material from other books without permission. Your writing also needs to be clear and concise, instructions easy to follow and unambiguous, and technical information has to be accurate.

You may have a small skill which everyone wants to learn: a 32-page booklet, *How To Flatten Your Stomach*, self-published by Jim Everroad sold well over a million copies in America. In Australia, Ron Edwards runs The Rams Skull Press which publishes small books on bushcraft — you will often find his books in shops specialising in self-sufficiency. He is selling information on old skills which have been nearly lost, and focuses on several skills per book and creating a series, rather than trying to gather them all at once into a large publication. This is more flexible, allowing him to add titles at any time, and also attractive to his customers. Ron also writes articles for *Earth Garden* magazine using material from these books, which is excellent publicity.

In New Zealand, Spinal Publications New Zealand Ltd publishes the patient self-treatment books entitled *Treat Your Own Back* and *Treat Your Own Neck* (now translated into thirteen languages), and *Treat Your Own Strains, Sprains & Bruises*, as well as professional texts, such as, *The Lumbar Spine Mechanical Diagnosis & Therapy* and *The Cervical & Thoracic Spine Mechanical Diagnosis & Therapy*. These titles are distributed internationally via agencies in Australia, USA, UK, Hong Kong, Germany, Benelux, Italy, Sweden and Switzerland.

Another growing area is teachers who are creating their own class materials and guides for students, either textbooks, workbooks, study notes or supplementary information. I have had students creating books who have been music teachers, calligraphy tutors, ESL teachers, and a woman who was teaching Ukrainian to 5–7-year-olds. Each of these people either had a special teaching method for which they needed written material, or were attempting to fill a gap where no suitable, commercially published books were available.

Making money

Some people will tell you that self-publishing is expensive, that you'll lose money, that the only book which can make a profit is the 'how-to' book. I believe if you plan properly and are realistic about how many books you can sell (and tailor your production process accordingly) you can at least earn your expenses back, if not make a small profit.

Of course, if you take writing time into account, then you probably won't make a profit, but there are many instances where ten per cent royalties from a commercial publisher didn't recompense writing time either.

You can make money in self-publishing if you act like a professional. If your print run will be in the thousands, you are going to be running a business. This means you have to wear yet another hat, that of bookkeeper or accountant. You will need to keep track of expenses and receipts right from the beginning and set up efficient financial reporting and paperwork. You will have to talk to the Tax Office about sales tax, issue invoices and receipts . . . you may want to hire an accountant if your venture warrants it. The question is, can you really sell that many books? I will never forget hearing about a man who had written a horror novel, à la Stephen King, and lost his house because he only managed to sell a few hundred out of several thousand copies. This could be you!

If you are realistic and plan well, it won't be. Sometimes you

Why are you doing it?

will learn the hard way and overextend, but being sensible will keep you out of debt. And the satisfaction of doing it yourself, having total creative control over design and production, is the biggest bonus.

2 The pros and cons of self-publishing

These days commercial publishing is a business — companies are getting bigger and the profit margin is very important. This means there are many books which have great merit, or particular niche audiences, which will not achieve commercial publication simply because they won't make enough money.

Poetry is a slightly different ballgame because some publishers have a poetry imprint for the prestige, and poetry collections are often subsidised by the Literature Fund of the Australia Council (as are many first and second novels), and in New Zealand by Creative New Zealand. However publishers don't expect to make a lot of money from poetry. Small presses, such as Pariah Press in Australia, and in New Zealand the publishers of *Spin*, *Takahe* and *Poetry New Zealand*, rely on author sales and grants to keep them afloat. Many distributors are reluctant to take on poetry, even from these prestigious small presses.

Some books, such as family or local histories, may have a limited audience, but it is an intensely interested one which means a small guaranteed number of sales — great for self-publishers but not viable for commercial ones. The area where self-publishers excel is in personal sales — poets sell at readings, handypersons sell at demonstrations and classes, travel writers sell at talks, and so on.

Self-publishing means that a much wider variety of books is available to readers. If we relied solely on books generally sold

The pros and cons of self-publishing

in bookshops, the range available would tend to become rather bland. Self-publishers ferret out new trends, new ideas, new kinds of writing, and see and fill the small gaps in the market better.

The advances in technology mean that self-publishing has never been more accessible, flexible or affordable. You no longer have to go to a printer and order a minimum number of copies to make the cost of plates and machine runs worthwhile. You can do very small print runs of 50 or less (although the unit cost will be higher). You can do your own typesetting, design and even physically bind the book yourself, all of which saves money. You can get your book out much faster than a commercial publisher (their average is 9 months to a year) and take advantage of coincidence or luck. When children's writer and illustrator, Michael Salmon, self-published his first picture book in Canberra, a photo appeared in the *Australian Women's Weekly* of the Prime Minister's wife reading his book to one of her offspring. Sales subsequently skyrocketed and he reprinted very quickly, then went on to produce two more before teaming up with a commercial publisher. Michael has always been a very active self-marketer and still visits hundreds of schools every year, selling and promoting his books.

When Ian Wishart published his book, *Paradise Conspiracy*, it ranked as one of the ten bestsellers in its first year of publication in New Zealand due to the author being the chief reporter in the controversial Winebox investigation.

You get to be the writer, editor, designer and publisher, make all the creative decisions, choose your own cover design and title and how the book will look. When a book is accepted for commercial publication, many of these decisions are taken out of your hands. You learn new skills of all kinds in a practical, hands-on way. Some people practise first with a very small book, such as eight poems or one story. This gives you a good indication of the work involved, as well as giving you a sense of how a whole book comes together, and shows the extra skills you might need to learn.

If you want to publish your own book, you can live anywhere. You don't have to reside in a major city, although this might mean you have easier access to printers and some technology.

Ron Edwards runs The Rams Skull Press from Kuranda in Northern Queensland.

If you are aiming at eventually having a book accepted by a large publisher, a venture into self-publishing can help to raise your profile as a writer and give you more confidence, as well as hands-on experience of the intricacies of publishing. Conversely, if you have been commercially published and your book has gone out of print, when the rights revert to you, you can republish it yourself (just make sure the market hasn't been exhausted).

These are some of the good points. On the down side, self-publishing can be a headache or an out-and-out nightmare. This manual is aimed at guiding you around some of the black holes waiting for you. At all times your catchwords should be *'Be Honest, Be Practical, Be Sensible'*. It is very easy to get swept away by fantasies of 'what if', and by stories of so and so who made a mint or was picked up by a big publisher. These are the exceptions and you will do well to remember it.

Those who have self-published before know how difficult it is to sell more than a couple of hundred copies of even the most attractive book. *If 60 per cent of your copies end up in boxes in your garage you haven't successfully self-published, no matter what your print run was.* In Australia and New Zealand we have much smaller populations spread over a huge land mass. People often overestimate their capacity to distribute and sell, and underestimate the travelling and time involved.

It's far better to do your groundwork, produce 200 copies and sell them all. You then have the money to reprint if you wish or, better still, go on to your next book! If you decide to reprint, you have the funds from sales to do so and you have the artwork ready to go again.

Another hole people fall into is underestimating the importance of a great cover and simple page design. If you want to sell your book, it must be of equal quality to other books in that price range. It must compete, be 'pick-uppable' and readable. I've seen covers bland enough to be confused with a notebook, and page design so fancy there was hardly any room for the text. You should be aware of the market in which you are competing.

The pros and cons of self-publishing

You need plenty of time to achieve successful publication and sales targets. If you have a full-time job and you want to sell 1500 copies, you'd better take plenty of leave. Printers, bookshops and libraries tend to work the same hours you do and are rarely willing to talk to salespeople at night or on weekends.

You also need money to pay your bills. Most of your costs will be payable before you actually sell any books, although you could arrange part-payments with your printer if he is amenable. If you're tempted to go for those expensive extras, can you pay for them? How?

You should choose a printing option which best suits your desired quality and your pocket. If you use a commercial printer, it needs to be one with whom you can communicate, who has printed books before instead of just stationery. The printer is running a business and you are just another customer. You should also educate yourself about the printing process involved and the terminology. The technology is here but you should understand how to use it to your best advantage. Some of this is covered in this book and will give you a working knowledge, but there are other texts which I have listed which will give you in-depth technical information if you need it.

The biggest problem any self-publisher faces is distribution and selling. Bookshops take 40 per cent of your cover price, distributors take another 20 per cent — most distributors won't take on self-published books anyway. So the main person who will be selling your book is YOU and if you don't feel comfortable about that, you will have to revise your plans. I have included a chapter on selling and marketing tactics because I think bookshops, for many people, aren't worth the effort. You're relying on someone else to sell for you who is also selling your competition. Hard but true.

If you're prepared to map out a comprehensive marketing plan and carry it through, spending three to four weeks doing nothing else, you'll be successful. Enthusiasm, energy and time are what is needed. But if you couldn't sell to a stranger or even a friend, consider instead a special limited edition for family and friends, a labour of love. You'll get just as much enjoyment and satisfaction out of it.

Whichever way you go, self-publishing is a great experience. You will learn a huge amount about all aspects of publishing, it's very creative and fulfilling to make it all happen yourself, and the resulting book will be a source of much pride.

3 Making initial decisions — The end before the beginning

In order to make decisions about production methods and print runs, you need to gather your information, do some research and survey the market. There's no point kidding yourself that you can sell hundreds of copies of your book when you don't like the marketing aspect of publishing. This is where you must be totally honest and realistic. Write it all down on paper, do your sums and think carefully.

Is it a feasible project?

Your dream may be a coffee-table book with 50 colour photos, glossy paper and a hard cover, but something like this could cost you over $30,000 for 1000 to 1200 copies. You have to decide if your book can be produced the way you want it without sending you broke. Moreover, can it be produced for a unit cost that will allow you to at least get your money back? You may have lots of money and aren't looking to even meet expenses, but you may still find that what you had in mind is out of your price range.

You may also need to pay others to do certain jobs such as typesetting or colour artwork. Is there a simpler way to manage these tasks? Could you learn the skills yourself, or modify your vision a little?

What kind of book is it?

Decide how you will define it, in one clear sentence. You will be asked this question many times and a short description will interest potential buyers. A long waffly rave will turn them off before you've even got the book printed. You can say, for example, 'It's a collection of my best poems from the past five years', or 'It's the story of my grandmother's life, including her favourite recipes'. If you can't define it, is it possible you have more than one book to publish? If your concept of it is very vague, you will have trouble making design decisions, writing blurbs and publicity material and selling it. Take the time now to find your book's focus.

Who will buy and read it?

We all have our own circle of family and friends who, even if they're not particularly interested in our subject matter or form, will buy a copy out of love or loyalty. If this is the limit of your buying audience, you may not even want to sell copies. They make great gifts.

If your list of potential buyers spreads further, write them all down. Members of your clubs, community groups, other poets at readings, and so on. If you include schools, libraries, local bookshops and newsagents, students and seminar attendees on your list, will you honestly be able to front up and present a sales pitch? Standing around with books in your hand and a hopeful look on your face will not work! You have to feel confident enough to SELL.

How will you reach these potential buyers? Have you got the time and energy to travel around and promote, give talks, keep up with the paperwork involved? Do you actually know what professional marketing requires?

Have you got a great title?

This is worth spending some time over if you haven't already decided on one. It needs to be the very best title you can come up with — one that won't date, or sound stupid, or mislead the buyer. It should fit the book and be one of your best selling points. A poetry or fiction title can be catchy or intriguing, but stay away from weird humour that only you appreciate! A non-fiction title should tell the reader what the book is about. Therefore *An Interesting Life on the Farm* sounds vague and could be anything, whereas *How To Run a Successful Hobby Farm* explains and entices.

You may need to check with *Books In Print* to see if your title has been previously used, not because titles are copyrighted (they're not, but trademarks are), but because another book recently published with your title might cause confusion. For example, *Oranges Are Not the Only Fruit* may seem like a great title for your fruit recipe book, but it is already the title of a very well-known novel by Jeanette Winterson, and the confusion would probably not be to your advantage. It will cause problems for booksellers and librarians for a start.

If you are having trouble with your title, try brainstorming on paper, writing down every idea, word and combination of words, then sifting through to select the best possibilities. Don't discard the use of a sub-title — sometimes they are necessary to properly indicate the scope of your book (like this one).

How many will you print?

When you have completed your list of buyers, make a realistic estimate of how many you think you can sell. I would suggest you then add no more than ten to twenty per cent to reach your final print run number.

There is absolutely no point in paying for 300 copies with a lovely colour cover (costing you a large amount of money) if you can't: a) sell them at a reasonable price to cover your costs; and b) sell at least 80 to 90 per cent of your copies. Your aim is to find that balance between quality and cost. If you want the option to reprint, make sure your production method allows for this in the simplest way possible (more on this in Chapters 7 and 12). Setting up for quick, efficient reprints is far better than ordering hundreds of extra copies 'just in case'.

There are some books which are always difficult to sell, simply because of preconceptions of the audience. Poetry and fiction are both likely to sell well in small print runs, but are rarely best sellers. Poetry tends to sell after people have heard or read some of it (remember Pam Ayres and her TV and radio exposure?), but you need to read well — it really helps. Fiction is very competitive and readers often don't like to take a punt on a new author so your publicity can play a huge role here. On the other hand, non-fiction and how-to books sell well if you can get them in front of your customers.

If you're not sure about the size of your market, you could devise a market research survey of your own. Don't just survey the general public, although that might be useful, but target clubs, organisations, schools, and so on who might already have an interest. You can ask questions about price, format and scope to help with your decision making. You'll get more honest answers if you make it anonymous.

How will you produce your book?

The answer to this is to be found in your answers to the first three questions. A small print run can often be largely produced by hand with the help of a high quality photocopier. If you are competing in the open market with hundreds or thousands of copies, then a good commercial printer is required because of the cover and binding. In between these options is a very feasible and economical compromise — a commercially printed cover with photocopied insides.

There are other formats which may suit your kind of book perfectly.

I have seen some lovely handwritten and crafted books, made from handmade paper and individually illustrated, bound and decorated. If you are producing a how-to book where clear diagrams on large pages are vital, something photocopied and comb-bound with a sturdy card cover will suffice, especially if it is sold by mail order and doesn't have to compete in bookshops.

Points to take into consideration include the necessity for a spine (i.e. perfect binding) for books intended for libraries and bookshops, any special production needs (such as, antique photo reproduction), and how many books you could reasonably hand bind on your own.

How much money do you have?

Obviously if you have very little, you're restricted to a photocopied book or just a few copies of something made by hand. Don't despair — it's good practice for your next, bigger project. If you have the finances, don't assume you need to spend it all. The printer might offer you a deal — $400 for an extra 200 copies. You can afford it, so why not? Because if it's 200 copies more than your realistic estimate of potential sales, you'll inevitably end up with 200 copies mouldering in your garage.

If you need more money and just don't have it, consider selling in advance to family and friends. Promise them the first copies, personally signed and numbered. That way you'll have funds and your first sales before you actually publish. Similiarly, if your book is about a subject such as growing orchids and you belong to an active orchid gardeners' club, you may be able to pre-sell to members or come to some arrangement for funds with the club.

It may also be possible to find a sponsor. One young woman I spoke to wanted to produce a collection of colour photos of the Amazon. The cost of such a book was well beyond her means, but she eventually found some sponsorship and went on to produce not only the book but also an exhibition of photographs.

I do not recommend you take out a loan. I'm sure that there are some who have, and been very successful, but it seems a foolhardy way to fund a book. If your customers are out there, they can be reached through early orders, special offers and effective publicity. And you would have to add bank interest to your unit cost, another extra.

You could also consider a joint venture, perhaps sharing a book with another poet, or working co-operatively with other self-publishers. Unfortunately there are currently no literature grants available for self-publishers in either Australia or New Zealand, and the Book Bounty will end on 31 December 1997.

Now that you've answered all these questions, you can analyse your position in terms of capacity to both publish and sell. The main thing at this point is to use your answers as the beginning of your publishing plan. Don't set everything in concrete — be prepared to be flexible, but don't make sensible decisions now and then get carried away later on (especially under the influence of over-optimistic friends!). Take the time to prepare a written plan, similar to the kind of business plan small business owners create, and regularly review it, using it as a guide.

An approximate timeline to take your book from first draft to sales follows. Some steps will be interchangeable, depending on your time and skills. It's difficult to estimate how long a book will take to get to printing stage, but if you are planning a reasonable print run and a marketing campaign, I would allow a minimum of three to six months. A small book which you will be producing on your computer and with a photocopier will need around two to three months. It depends on how complicated your production schedule will be.

Timeline

- Start a business file — collect receipts, price lists, etc. (for research costs at first, then later for costs and quotes).
- Write your book — rewrite as necessary. Type.
- Begin your analysis of readers and markets.
- Write away for permissions and any other extra material you need.
- Organise editing assistance — either friends, colleagues or a professional.
- Work on final, edited draft.
- Select final title and define your book.
- Organise typesetting or desktop publishing if required, including choice of typefaces, interior page design, book size, etc.
- Get quotes on your printing options.
- Work out your unit cost and retail price.
- Revise your production methods if you need to save money. Double-check your budget and costings.
- Proofread the final copy including headings and captions. Finalise design decisions.

Making initial decisions

- Organise interior artwork — illustrations, diagrams, etc.
- From market and reader analysis, make decisions on cover design, binding, print run. Review your finances and match to analysis and decisions.
- Organise extra funds, sponsors, subscriptions, if necessary. Or trim costs.
- Design your cover (or hire a designer).
- Prepare your marketing plan and early publicity.
- Write blurb and bio note — get a good photo of yourself.
- Ring the National Library for your ISBN.
- Ring D.W. Thorpe — in New Zealand, c/o Heinemann Reference (Reed Publishing (NZ) Ltd) — to receive forms for *Books In Print*.
- Apply for your barcode if necessary.
- Register your business name if you want one. Talk to an accountant.
- Proofread galleys very carefully, and check placement of illustrative material and captions.
- Prepare contents and index if necessary, using page numbers on galleys.
- Proofread contents and index.
- Get your book printed, whichever way you have decided.
- Prepare full promotional materials and order forms. Begin pre-publicity.
- Organise a Post Office box for orders if necessary.
- Contact distributors if required.
- Organise launch venue, launcher and catering. Ask friends and family to help. Check with printer that books are on schedule.
- Collect books from printer — check for damage or mistakes.
- Confirm your contracted distributor and supply with books.
- Send out review copies and a copy to your launcher.
- Send out launch invitations.
- Follow up on publicity and begin full campaign. Contact media and supply with promotional package if required.
- Organise speaking or reading engagements.
- Attend launch.
- Follow up on media coverage and begin engagements.
- Implement full marketing plan.

- Review progress and sales on a regular basis. Keep up with paperwork.
- Decide if a reprint is necessary. Organise quickly and keep things moving.
- Review publishing venture and have a rest before the next one.

4 *Writing and editing*

Writing begins with ideas and research — where you go from there is up to you, depending on what kind of book you are writing. There are several tools which will come in very handy for you, no matter what your material or genre is. The first is a good dictionary and, given that you will be publishing in Australia, a big Macquarie dictionary is recommended (not the pocket size). You may also find a thesaurus useful. I prefer *Roget's Thesaurus*, but this tends to be a personal choice. If you have trouble with grammar and punctuation, you could begin with *The Elements of Style* (William Strunk Jnr and E.B. White) which covers the basics, and go on to a professional style guide when you're ready.

Only you will know the kind of research required for your particular book. If family history is your interest, you may want to join a genealogical society or attend a class on how to get started on your fact-finding mission. The place where most people begin is the Public Record Office (Public Reference Enquiries can be made in Australia on (03) 9360 9665, or freecall from country areas 1 800 657 452). If you are planning to use the library, take the time to learn how to use the catalogue and Dewey classification system. For journal articles you may be able to use the *Reader's Guide to Periodical Literature* to find what you want. It will also pay to become friendly with your librarians so that, once they are familiar with your quest, they will be able to assist you more easily. If your local public library is under-resourced (and so many are now), try using the library at your nearest tertiary institution. Sometimes they won't allow you to borrow but it's worth asking.

Where possible, check your facts and figures in more than one source. I have known of people who have found three or four different versions of the same incident or details. If you can't ascertain which is correct, choose the one that correlates best with your other information and add a note, perhaps a footnote, regarding the other versions. Use your judgement about anecdotal material, especially where you might offend someone.

Should you use a computer?

There are many people who still shy away from computers and certainly, if you only plan to produce one book, it wouldn't be to your advantage to go through the hassle of buying a computer and learning how to use it just for that (although it's a good excuse!). Paying someone else to typeset your book will probably be cheaper and simpler in the long run. Some of the reasons you might want to consider purchasing a computer include:

- We are getting more technological every day, not less. This applies especially to the printing industry, where you can now give your printer a book on disk with no paste-ups required. When a book is on disk, reprints become fast and simple as well. Also you can make late corrections if they are necessary.
- It is possible to buy a second-hand computer now for $500 to $800, one that will run all the basic software you require. This reduction in cost, as the technology gets faster and can accomplish more, is a bonus to the writer and self-publisher who usually only needs good word processing or simple desktop publishing software. I still use Windows 3.1 and Word 6, even though there are newer versions around, because they do all I require. Another advantage of this cheaper hardware is that you can then often afford a high quality laser printer, and even these are dropping in price all the time. Note: Before buying a laser printer, check the cost of replacement toner cartridges and whether they can be recycled or not.

Writing and editing

- Using a computer and word-processing program makes rewriting and editing a breeze. Corrections can be done with the click of a few keys, paragraphs and whole sections can be moved around and most programs allow you to see your typefaces on the screen as they will be printed out. You are able to produce your manuscript in 12 point and double-spaced for easy reading and editing, then change it later into the way you want it to look in your printed book.
- It will save you money and time on editing, typesetting and designing, and when you are using professionals, time is money. A handwritten manuscript will take a typist or typesetter much longer to decipher and more mistakes are likely. Once the final editing is completed, you can hand your disk to the designer for the next stage. This is what I did with my poetry manuscript, *Edge*. The designer showed me sample typefaces (using some of my poems as examples), we decided on heading and text styles and he completed all the design on his computer, using my disk. It was quick, simple and much cheaper.
- You can use your computer for your records (such as, income and expenditure, tax records, invoices and receipts, mailouts and publicity material) and create a database of prospective customers.
- If you are more technologically minded, you can buy a bigger computer and modem, connect to the Internet and use it for research and advertising purposes.

The eternal question is always what kind of computer should I buy? IBM compatible or MacIntosh? It's a debate that's been raging for years and there is no clear answer. For some, it's better to have the same type of computer at home as they use at work or school. For others it's a matter of which one you first used and feel comfortable with, or price. There are books and magazines around which compare the two and may help you choose. Try both out, preferably at work or through friends, and don't listen to the salesmen's patter. Or, should I say, listen to who talks to you properly and explains in a way you understand. There are rather a lot of young salesmen whose main aim in life seems to be to make you feel as inferior and stupid as possible. Always ask about after-sales help and service.

For the purposes of this book, I define word processing as basically keying in your text, using simple headings, page numbers, double spacing and so on (so your manuscript comes out the way you'd present it to a commercial publisher for consideration). Desktop publishing is taking this simply formatted manuscript and transforming it into a book, so when you print it out on your own laser printer the pages will look like the finished product.

Editing

The writing and editing in your self-published book must be the best you can do, and then it should be even better. The last thing you want is readers noticing mistakes or poor writing and then saying, 'Oh well, it's only self-published'. You know yourself how offputting it is to read a book which has obviously not been given that critical eye and final polish.

Before you ask outside readers of any kind to comment on your manuscript, you should edit it yourself to the best of your ability. Achieving the required distance from your writing is difficult. In order to do this, you should put your manuscript away for several weeks to help you gain a 'fresh eye' for it. Then begin by looking at the following aspects:

- Have you found that perfect title yet? If you're still wrestling with several choices, road-test them with friends and acquaintances to help you select the best one.
- Does the opening catch the reader's interest? Are they going to want to keep reading, drawn in by your first words? In a children's book, the first sentence should get them in. Your first poem in a collection should be one of your strongest.
- Does your book fulfil its promise? In fiction, all those elements of character, plot, theme, and dialogue should be working together in a sound structure. In poetry, you should have weeded out all the weaker poems and given careful thought to the order. Poems wrongly placed can alter the whole tone and sense of the book. A non-fiction book should tell readers

Writing and editing

concisely and clearly what they want to know, with effective use of headings and sub-headings. It should be well organised, with material in the right order.
- Does your conclusion work?
- Is your material accurate? Even in fiction, if you have errors in your background material, such as a street out of place or the wrong king's name, you will undermine that 'suspension of disbelief' which allows the reader to enter your fictional world. In non-fiction, errors will undermine the credibility of your whole book.
- Are your paragraphs working? Are your sentences well constructed and of varying lengths to avoid dullness?
- Is your spelling, punctuation and grammar correct? Have you stuck to your style guide? Use your spell checker and dictionary. It might pay to ask a friend to help with your corrections if you are planning to hire an editor. It will save time and money later if your editor doesn't have to spend hours on these kinds of corrections.
- Is your manuscript printed out on clean paper, with clear print and double spacing? This makes it much easier for everyone to read.

You may want to consult more books at this point to help you in the writing and editing process (see 'General references' in Appendix 3).

There are several ways in which you can get critical feedback. If you are in a writing group, ask for a higher level of workshopping and comment than you would perhaps normally receive. You may only be able to ask them to look at two or three chapters, but you can apply their comments to the rest of the work. You can also ask friends with experience to read your manuscript and comment. Don't ask people who don't read, or aren't capable of separating the text from you personally. This usually rules out family members and close friends!

Ask them to be specific in their comments. They should point out what isn't clear, any queries they have, what they didn't like and why. Ask them also to be brutally honest but don't argue or get upset when they are. Take a few days to calm down, then look at the manuscript critically with their comments in mind and consider all aspects. Remember that these people are all your first readers, your sample audience, and they can help you iron out problems before the book goes out to a wider audience who will be paying for the privilege and want their money's worth.

If you have no-one who can give you good critical feedback, one option is the manuscript assessment service offered by the National Book Council. Assessors are anonymous but all are professional writers or editors. They will assess fiction, poetry, children's books and non-fiction. Rates vary from $100.00 for a children's manuscript up to 30,000 words, up to $250.00 for a 100,000 word novel. For your money, you will receive a written assessment (on average four to five pages) which will tell you where your strengths are and what isn't working. Most importantly, the assessor will say whether your book is ready to submit to a publisher, which for self-publishers means is it good enough to stand up in the marketplace. This assessment does not include editing; it is a general critique. In New Zealand, TFS Literary Agency and Manuscript Assessment Service, PO Box 29–023, Ngaio, Wellington, works with writers of fiction, non-fiction and children's books. Rates vary from $90 for 5000 words; $168.75 for scripts between 5000 and 10,000 words. For each additional 10,000 words up to 70,000 words add $56.25. For each additional 10,000 words over 70,000 add $39.38.

You may wish to hire a professional editor, particularly if you intend to compete in the commercial market with your book. This could be expensive so get quotes first. Freelance editors should look at the manuscript first so they can estimate the number of hours required to edit properly. If your manuscript is in a mess or needs lots of work, it will cost you more. The recommended rate is $30 to $40 per hour, depending on the complexity of the job and the experience of the editor. It is sensible to provide prospective editors with a brief outlining your requirements.

An editor will give you professional, independent, unbiased criticism. They will point out inconsistencies, repetitions, 'woolliness' and disorganised material. When you are too close to your writing, there are many things you just can't see for yourself. If you have devised your own style sheet, make sure your editor has a copy of this. Discuss your needs with your editor, decide what you want done and confirm it in writing, including the maximum cost. Don't be overawed — make sure you find an editor to whom you can talk confidently and freely, who understands what you want to do.

You can obtain a register of freelance editors from the Society of Editors in each State, or the Book Editors Association of New Zealand. These will list editors in your geographical area as well as those who edit specialist publications. The register entries will tell you the qualifications of each person and what other publications they have worked on. Some editors are also able to provide design and typesetting services, or can refer you to reliable professionals they have worked with.

Editors' societies

Australian Capital Territory
PO Box 3222
Manuka
ACT 2603

New South Wales
PO Box 254
Broadway
NSW 2007.

Queensland
PO Box 1524
Toowong
Qld 4066.

South Australia
PO Box 2328
Kent Town
SA 5071.

Tasmania
PO Box 32
Sandy Bay
Tas 7005.

Victoria
PO Box 176
Carlton South
Vic 3053.

Western Australia
PO Box 908
Nedlands
WA 6009.

New Zealand
PO Box 99259
Newmarket
Auckland.

While you are in the editing process, make sure you have started to gather all the other material you will need, such as photos, diagrams, maps, and and don't forget to apply for any permissions needed (see Chapter 5 on how to go about this). Keep a record of what you need and mark each item off as you receive it, then store it carefully. You may want to write your captions and chapter headings now, if you haven't already done so, and begin compiling your bibliography, glossary, appendices and indexing headings. Check that you have the correct information to write captions for your photographs. Family photos are notorious for including anonymous people whom no-one recognises. Check spellings of all names, places and dates.

Probably the most important point to keep in mind about writing and editing your book is to put your ego to one side. You are publishing for a buying audience, and in order to make them feel their money was well-spent, your writing and editing must be topnotch. It is a job that very few people do well on their own.

Note: If the book which is being published is an anthology from your writing group or club, you should work out how the selection of material and editing is to happen. Some contributors may need much more editing than others — how will this be handled tactfully but firmly? If the policy is that everyone gets to have a piece of writing included, try to ensure a high level of quality. Will you appoint one or two people as supervising editors? Try to sort out and agree to all these details before you start, and maybe avoid bloodshed! Or at least a feud which might last for years (I kid you not).

5 Some important technicalities

As the publisher, it is your responsibility to ensure that you are on safe legal ground with your book. This applies to aspects which are favourable to you, such as your copyright and ISBN, as well as those which may turn out to be very unfavourable if you don't deal with them, such as permissions and libel.

If you are not sure about any of these issues, enquire further with the appropriate body. There are so many different kinds of books, each with its own approach and subject area, that it would be impossible to cover everything here.

Copyright

There is no need for you to register copyright of your book with anyone. As soon as you write it, it is automatically protected. Although this is recognised, you should place the copyright symbol and year of publication on your work (on the back of the title page), e.g. © Jill Smith 1997. It operates as a warning that you understand your rights and ensures full international protection.

You can also place a copyright notice in the same place, which outlines your conditions. As an example, it might read:

> *This book is copyright. Apart from any fair dealing for the purpose of study, research, criticism, review, or as otherwise permitted under the Copyright Act, no part may be reproduced*

by any process without written permission. Inquiries should be directed to the author.

Copyright generally lasts from the time the material was created until 50 years after the author's death. In Europe it has just been increased to 70 years. You cannot copyright your ideas, only the form your ideas take, e.g. your written words. One way to establish proof of your copyright is to keep early drafts of your work and date them. It also pays to print out and keep hard copies rather than leaving everything on disk. You also cannot copyright a title, so it might be a good idea to check a current edition of *Books In Print* in case your wonderful poetry title happens to be the same as that for a book on footrot in cows!

Self-publishers generally are writing and producing books in their own time. If yours was written in the course of paid employment, your copyright might actually belong to your employer. If in doubt, check. You can obtain more detailed and specialised information from the Australian Copyright Council, Suite 3, 245 Chalmers St, Redfern NSW 2016. Phone (02) 9318 1788 or toll free (008) 226 103. In New Zealand contact the Copyright Council of New Zealand Inc., PO Box 5028, Wellington. Phone (04) 472 4430.

Permissions

Copyright works in the other direction as well. Therefore you cannot use portions of other people's work and claim it as your own. You may quote a small amount from a book or an article, as long as you include author and title. Small means a paragraph from a book or a few lines from an article. You cannot use a line from a poem or song without permission.

If you are in any doubt about this, it's better to be safe and acquire a written permission from the author involved. This needs to be done very early on as it may take several months to receive a reply.

You should write to the publisher to request the permission, and it's a good idea to actually provide a standard letter which can be signed and returned. Your letter should include the title, author and type of book you are publishing, the estimated date of publication and print run, the title and author of the work from which you wish to quote, its publication date, the page(s) on which the material appears, the total number of words, a copy of the exact quote, a statement to say the permission will cover any and all editions, and a request for how the copyright holder wishes the acknowledgement to read (see sample Fig 5.1 on page 38). Send two copies of this letter so the holder can keep a copy for themselves. Enclose a stamped, self-addressed envelope to encourage a quick reply.

If you don't hear within a month or two, follow it up, otherwise you might end up holding back publication while you wait and wait. Sometimes a fee may be requested. It's up to you to decide if it's worth your while to pay it. If you need more than one or two permissions, keep track of them all with a log book so you can see what is outstanding.

You will find that some works are in the public domain, but don't assume that because something is very old, it will be freely usable. Some long-dead writers have their copyrights renewed by their estates. Always check. If you want to know more about copyright, contact the Australian Copyright Council or the Copyright Council of New Zealand. They provide general information, but also publish booklets on copyright in specific areas such as family histories.

Illustrations, maps, diagrams, paintings and photos

All of these are protected by copyright, just as your words are. So you can't take them out of other books and use them as you please. Like quotes, you need permission from their creators. It is your responsibility to track them down. It may be easier in the long run to create your own, unless the material is vital and can't be reproduced, e.g. historical photos or maps. In Australia and New Zealand, the copyright in photographs continues to exist for 50 years after first publication.

In the case of illustrations, you may be able to draw your own or you may have a friend who is a good artist. Clear, well-defined line drawings are best, especially if you are photocopying. Black and white photos need to be scanned or bromided. Anything in colour will cost you more — full colour will cost you a lot. At this point in time, colour photocopying is not a cheap option.

Books of copyright free illustrations are available in specialist bookshops. If you decide to use these, be sparing. There are also files of pictures on the various computer programs which are copyright free but they are so commonly used that they are not recommended.

If you want to reproduce a painting, perhaps on your cover, remember that the copyright resides with the painter, not the current owner of the painting.

Quotes

Many famous or familiar quotations are in the public domain, but again it's better to check than be sorry later. If you want to use a quote by someone famous which applies to an aspect of your book, e.g. a quote from the Prime Minister about a political or racial issue, write and ask permission. You may find it helpful to prepare a synopsis of your book so the person concerned understands where and how their quote will be used. Allow plenty of time for a reply.

ISBN and ISSN registration

I would recommend that every book you publish which you intend to sell should have an ISBN (International Standard Book Number). Magazines should have an ISSN (International Standard Serial Number). You apply to Thorpe Bibliographic Services for these. The ISBN and ISSN Agency can be contacted on: Phone: (03) 9245 7397; Fax: (03) 9245 7395; or email: isbn.agency@thorpe.com.au. In New Zealand Contact the ISBN Librarian or ISSN Librarian at the National Library of New Zealand: Phone: (04) 474 3090; Fax: (04) 474 3161; or email: ISSN@natlib.govt.nz.

The ISBN Agency will want to know the title, author, publisher's name and address and date of publication (which will probably be your launch date). They may also want to know the number of pages. You should place your ISBN on the back of

Some important technicalities

your title page (see Chapter 8), along with your other publishing information. You can also print it on the back cover and/or spine of your book. It must be printed exactly as given, especially the spaces.

From this, your book will be listed in the *Australian National Bibliography*. Bookbuyers, bookshops and library suppliers can track you down through this if they want a copy, but it is even better to have it listed in *Books In Print*, published by D.W. Thorpe in Melbourne. You should contact them by phoning (03) 9245 7370 and they will send you out the forms to be filled in.

In return for your ISBN or ISSN, you must send a copy of your book to the National Library and State Library in your State for legal deposit. The National Library will send you a Legal Deposit receipt number in reply. In some States you need to send copies to other libraries as well, such as the Parliamentary Library. The National Library will advise you of legal deposit requirements in your State.

You can also get Cataloguing-in-Publication information from the CiP Unit at the National Library of Australia, phone: (06) 262 1458. This service is free and available for self-published books.

In New Zealand, contact the National Library of New Zealand in Wellington for ISBN and cataloguing information. Phone (04) 474 3090. Self-publishers are also encouraged to lodge a copy of their book with the Alexander Turnbull Library Heritage Section.

Bar codes

Nearly every commercially published book today has a bar code printed on its back cover. Bar codes and their accompanying EAN (European Article Number) are part of a worldwide system which identifies products, shipments of goods, services, companies and organisations and locations by giving each one a unique number. The bar code represents the EAN in a form which can be scanned and entered into a computer. It allows shops to keep track of stock and sales very efficiently.

You would probably only want to acquire a bar code and EAN

for your book if you intended selling quite a number of copies through retail outlets. You need to pay a membership fee of $100 to EAN Australia, who administer the system and allocate numbers and bar codes. This is a yearly fee which covers all numbers and bar codes you require. In addition, for books and magazines you need to advise them of your ISBN or ISSN numbers.

You can contact EAN Australia on 1300 366 033 for further information and application forms. EAN New Zealand is in Wellington, phone (04) 499 4838.

Publishing under a business name

You may decide that you don't want to publish under your own name — you want to use a trading name. Some people feel it makes them look more professional, others actually want to obscure the fact that their book is self-published. It is quite simple and not too expensive to register a trading name.

You need to apply to the Office of Fair Trading & Business Affairs (or equivalent in your State or country) to register your chosen name. You may not use a trading name that someone else has, and staff will check their database to ensure your name is available. In Victoria, the cost is $70 for three years, and $50 to renew every three years after that. Your main obligations are to begin trading within two months of registration, with the intention of making a profit. Dealing with income tax is your responsibility and you should use an accountant to clarify details such as tax returns and sales tax. If you decide to discontinue your trading name, you must apply to the Office for cancellation.

Book Bounty

Book Bounty acts like a printing subsidy for Australian books. It has been gradually whittled down over the past few years and as of 31 December 1997 will end. There are restrictions, such as a minimum print run of 1000 copies and minimum production costs of $3700. For many small publishers, Book Bounty is more trouble than it is worth, as it forces you into high print runs and costs.

Some important technicalities

Plagiarism

Plagiarism is taking someone else's work and passing it off as your own. There have been some very famous cases in the past few years. It is definitely not a recommended practice!

Libel

The laws on libel continue to be rather tortuous but, put as simply as possible, you libel someone if you hold them up to ridicule or contempt, or damage their reputation. The defence of truth does not always operate so do not rely on it. If you have any doubts whatsoever in this area, seek legal advice.

The main thing to remember is that you have entire responsibility and liability for what you publish, so you will be the one being sued. If you're worried about offending someone, send them a printout of your book to read. If they threaten to sue, you are forewarned, which is better than appearing in court afterwards. If your printer decides he doesn't want to print your book, either because it's defamatory or obscene, you have no comeback.

For initial advice and referrals, contact the Arts Law Centre in Sydney (02) 9356 2566, or similar arts law referral services in your State. In New Zealand, contact a local Citizens Advice Bureau for a referral to a community law centre in your area.

Publishing on the Internet

You may well find that the Internet is a great place to publicise your book. You can set up your own Home Page, publish a short excerpt to tempt people and provide an email address for orders. How are you going to collect the money?

This is only one issue you will have to contend with, because it means you will be getting into credit card transactions and security. On the other hand, if you decide to publish your whole book on your Home Page, you have no control over copyright. Anyone can take any or all of the text and illustrations and use your material any way they please. It is possible for you to find out if your material is being used by someone else on the Internet by doing a search through a search engine. Try http://www.altavista.com. The issues of copyright and moral rights are currently being debated with no solutions in sight.

While there are now programs which provide templates for creating Home Pages, so you don't need to learn the coding, they will continue to be a little like all of the other templates — they all look the same after a while. And how will you get your Home Page noticed? How will you get people to come and visit it?

This whole area continues to grow and diversify at such a rate that many of these problems may be easily solved in a year or two. If it is something you think will suit your book, take the time to investigate it thoroughly.

Public Lending Right

This is something you won't need to worry about until after your book is published and has sold quite a few copies, mainly because of its restrictions.

Public Lending Right (PLR) was established to compensate authors for their books held in public libraries, which readers borrow instead of buying. The rate of payment is approved each year by the Minister of Communications and the Arts — in 1996 the rate per book was $1.173 for creators and $0.293 for publishers.

The restrictions are:

- you must be an Australian citizen or normally residing in Australia
- you must be an eligible creator i.e. author, illustrator, editor, translator, etc.
- you must be entitled to receive royalties from the sale of your book
- your book must have an ISBN, be offered for sale and have no more than five creators.

You are eligible to apply if you are a self-publisher, but 50 or more copies of your book must be held in libraries in Australia. Claims for payment close on 30 June each year.

You can get more information from the Public Lending Right

Some important technicalities

Scheme, GPO Box 3241, Canberra ACT 2601. Phone (06) 279 1650 or (toll free) 1800 672842.

Educational Lending Right was intended to be an extension of PLR, to compensate authors for books held in educational libraries. It was due to begin in 1996. Unfortunately, at the time of writing, the federal government had decided to cancel ELR — writers and publishers are still protesting.

A similar scheme to PLR operates in New Zealand, and is called the Authors' Fund. It is administered by Creative New Zealand (the arts council). It is not payable to New Zealand writers living outside of the country, or to beneficiaries after the author's death. Information and application forms can be obtained from New Zealand Authors' Fund, Creative New Zealand, PO Box 3806, Wellington. Phone (04) 473 0880, Fax (04) 471 2865.

Selling other rights

Your book may be suitable for publishing in other mediums, either in full or as an extract. You could sell an excerpt to a magazine or another publisher for an anthology, or the whole text to radio or television. Or your book might be suitable for transferring on to CD-ROM.

Each of these areas involves knowledge and experience which I am not able to detail here. Consult your writers' organisations (such as the Fellowship of Australian Writers or the Australian Society of Authors), an arts lawyer, or perhaps even an agent if appropriate.

Copyright Agency Limited (CAL)

CAL is a not-for-profit company that represents the print copyright interests of thousands of publishers, authors and print journalists in Australia.

CAL has been authorised by the Federal Attorney General as the declared collecting society for the administration of the statutory licence for certain types of copying by education institutions. On behalf of its members, CAL has entered into copying agreements with the Federal and State governments for certain types of print copying by other organisations including corpora-

> **Figure 5.1 Sample permission letter**
>
> 24 March 1997
>
> RE: PERMISSION TO REPRINT MATERIAL
>
> Dear _____
>
> I am currently writing a book titled *Life in Early Maryborough*, which is a family history. I intend to publish it in September this year. I will be printing 200 copies, and most of these will be sold to interested family members and people in the area.
>
> I would like your permission to include the diagram and excerpt outlined below in any and all editions of my book. I also include a photocopy of the material for your information. A full acknowledgement of your material would be provided in whatever form you feel suitable; sample wording has been included below.
>
> I enclose a duplicate copy of this letter for your records and a stamped, self-addressed envelope for your reply. Thank you in advance for your assistance and prompt response.
>
> Yours sincerely,
>
> *Material to be reprinted:*
> *From:* (title of book or source publication)
> *Author/Editor:*
> *Year of publication:*
> *Page reference:*
> *Description of extract:*
> *Number of words in extract:*
> *Proposed acknowledgement wording (to be amended if required):* (provide an example which the copyright owner can then change if they want to)

tions, press clipping services and non-profit organisations. In response to the changing needs of both creators and users, CAL has also recently developed licences for certain types of digital copying, including copying onto new media products such as CD-ROM, and on-line copying.

If you are a member, CAL will collect fees for licenced copying on your behalf and distribute those monies to you, less

Some important technicalities

administrative expenses, according to surveys of users' copying practices.

Membership is free, so if you think your book is likely to be copied, it would be worth joining. A full information kit can be obtained from CAL, Level 19, 157 Liverpool St, Sydney NSW 2000. Phone (02) 9394 7600, Fax (02) 9394 7601 or e-mail: info@copyright.com.au. Further details can also be obtained from CAL's website at URL http://www.copyright.com.au

(*This information and wording supplied by CAL*)

Copyright Licensing Limited (CLL)

CLL is a non-profit organisation established by the Book Publishers Association of New Zealand (BPANZ). On behalf of its owner, BPANZ and the New Zealand Society of Authors the organisation licenses the reproduction of extracts from printed copyright works. The major users of copyright text are from three major sectors — government, education and industry. The proceeds from licensing and royalties are distributed to the owners after a deduction for administration costs.

6 *Typesetting and proofreading*

Once your manuscript is edited, you're ready for the next step. A few years ago, all printed books were phototypeset which was a time-consuming and costly process. Today this process is still available as an option and will produce very high quality printable text, but rates can be anything from $25 an hour and upward.

This is one area where technology is a real bonus to the self-publisher. Anyone can typeset their own book on a home computer and print out a laser copy which will produce a quality product. Or you can prepare your manuscript on a disk and take it to the printers who can convert it to their technology. We are making further advances in this area all the time, so that printing and publishing are becoming cheaper and more accessible. If your book is a reasonable size (more than 100 pages) or you are planning to publish more than one title, you should seriously consider buying a computer. It doesn't have to be brand new and expensive, as an old 386 or 486 will run an efficient word processing program and a laser printer.

Using a typewriter

If you don't have access to a computer and laser printer, and can't afford typesetting, you can still use a typewriter. Important points to keep in mind are:

Typesetting and proofreading

- Use a new ribbon to get the darkest possible print — even better, use a typewriter with a one-use-only carbon ribbon.
- Make sure your page size is correct, e.g. type A5 pages on half of A4, and allow good margins.
- Be aware that typing will use up more space as there is no kerning or automatic space reduction between letters, and corrections will be tedious.
- Be aware that you will have very little latitude for typeface variety — you may have to use Letraset or similar products for titles and headings.

Using a computer and printer

You don't need to use Pagemaker or Quark (desktop publishing software) in order to typeset your book. Word or Wordperfect, or similar programs, will be perfectly adequate. With these, you are able to set your margins, automatic page numbering, use different typefaces for headings and different sized typefaces and spacing for text. Some points to remember are:

- Don't go overboard with your typefaces and decorative additions. A printer once told me a good rule of thumb was to use no more than three typefaces on a document — less is better. A good option is to choose one typeface and use the bold and italics for variety.
- Don't use a dot matrix printer — even 24 pins. The minimum print quality to aim for should be 600dpi laser. I have yet to see a bubble jet printer which provides the necessary quality of printout, even at 600dpi. This is because the ink 'bleeds' around the edges of the letters and is also susceptible to moisture and smudging. However, the quality of these printers is improving all the time. They are good for colour work, so you can print colour pictures to insert as you bind.
- Don't rely on the spelling check function to correct your mistakes. It won't pick up when you've wrongly used 'their/there', for example, or 'looping' instead of 'loping'.

It is possible for a reasonably experienced computer user to prepare the complete manuscript of their book, including all camera-ready copy and artwork. Photos and illustrations can be scanned in, text typeset with gutter allowances for binding, diagrams and tables added — you name it, a computer set up with the right software and a high resolution laser printer can do nearly everything.

It is also possible to make a mess of it and end up with something overdone, inaccurate and amateurish. My best advice in order to avoid this is to look at what works in other books, and what looks awful. If you're not sure of your own taste (whether others will like what you like), show examples to your friends and family and ask for honest opinions. 'Keep It Simple' is always an excellent rule to use which will help keep you out of the mire.

Some commercial printers have now advanced to using machines which don't require plates and look like a cross between a photocopier and a computer (see Chapter 7). You don't need to supply your manuscript on paper at all. Instead you hand over a computer disk and your book is printed from that. It's another advance which saves you money and allows easy reprints.

Sometimes there will be elements in your book which won't translate on disk. These can include photos, diagrams, tables and maps. If you are planning to prepare your book on disk, check with your printer first for software compatibility and any possible complications.

Using a professional typist or typesetter

If at all possible, you should do your own typesetting to save money if nothing else. However, that is impossible for some people to manage and they must pay for it instead. Prices for typing range from $20 per 1000 words to $3 to $4 per A4 double-spaced page. If you are providing a handwritten manuscript to be typed, it will cost you more if it's not very legible, and the typist is liable to make more mistakes.

Typesetting on computer (not phototypesetting) and/or desktop (DT) publishing will cost more and depends on what your book contains. Sixty pages of poems will cost less than sixty pages of dense text. As a guide, I have been quoted $10 per page or $50

Typesetting and proofreading

an hour, depending on the material being typeset. You can then have the copy put on a disk, printed out on a laser printer and with illustrations scanned in, all of which can then be taken to a printer. Like printing, this is an area where you need to shop around and get quotes. Have samples of your writing and what you want the pages to look like so the DT publisher can quote accurately and easily.

Desktop publishing has created a new area between typesetters (who deal in setting text, headings and captions) and book designers (who make the pages readable and pleasing to the eye, and often design the cover as well). There are a number of small businesses now who specialise in desktop publishing and often do books and manuals. Their final copy will usually be laser printed to a high quality but they may not be able to handle colour separations or complicated work. You can also desktop publish your own book at home to a similar standard, providing you have the expertise and equipment.

Phototypesetting provides excellent quality; a professional typesetting and artwork house can take your text and art (photos, maps, etc) and produce topnotch, camera-ready paste-ups for your printer which will make your book indistinguishable from a commercially published one. But it will cost you. Heaps. If you have the money and that is your aim, the same applies — shop around and get quotes. In this area you can save money in your preparation. Make sure everything you provide is correct, complete and your instructions are easy to understand. Anything which will take time to rectify or clarify will cost you. One way to assist the process is to make up your own style sheet for the typesetter to follow (see Style Guides 6.1 on page 45 and 8.1 on page 64).

Finally, make sure that what is going to be supplied to your printer for making the plates is fully completed and is what is expected. You need to liaise between the art house and the printer to ensure there are no misunderstandings.

Style Guides

The most commonly used style guide in Australia is probably

the *Style Manual: For authors, editors and printers*, published by the Australian Government Publishing Service. It is quite extensive, covering writing and editing, preparing copy for printing and information on publishing and bookmaking. It has plenty of examples and illustrations, and is used by many teachers in professional writing and editing courses. Another one is *The Cambridge Australian English Style Guide* by Pam Peters (Cambridge University Press).

In New Zealand the most commonly used style guides are *Style Book: A Guide for New Zealand Writers and Editors* (GP Publications) and *Write Edit Print: Style Manual for Aotearoa New Zealand* (AGPS Press & Lincoln University Press).

Many publishers provide their authors with their own style guides for preparation of manuscripts. One good reason for using a style guide, apart from correcting your grammar and punctuation, is to ensure consistency throughout the book. While you may choose to spell 'colour' as 'color', or 'utilise' as 'utilize', to use both versions in your book looks like an error.

I recommend you make up your own style sheet, for your reference as well as others, such as proofreaders. This will stipulate the consistent use of abbreviations, punctuation, spelling (which dictionary you will stick to), how dates and numbers will be written, how quotes will be set out, how other references will be cited, how words will be hyphenated, etc. All of this can be found in a professional style guide, but if you make up your own sheet and add to it as necessary, it will save a lot of time flicking through pages looking for the right rule or example.

Proofreading

I recommend to self-publishers that they use three proofreaders. This may sound like a lot but even with three, mistakes may still slip through. However, my three each have a different function.

The first reader looks for major and minor structural mistakes — repeated sentences, paragraphs and chapters out of order, general glitches that happen in the typesetting. You can ask anyone who is an interested and careful reader.

The second proofreader looks for spelling, punctuation and

Typesetting and proofreading

Figure 6.1 Style Sheet

A-D	E-H
Dr	handwritten (1 word)
camera ready	Home Page
Docutech	
disk	

I-L	M-P
Kwik Kopy	pick-up
inquiry	NSW

Q-T	U-Z
quick printer (2 words)	utilise (-ise)
Times Roman	
typeface (one word)	

grammar mistakes. Someone who is an English teacher, for example, might be good at this. Your final proofreader needs to be something of an expert, even pickier than No. 2, and you may want to pay for a professional. Rates range from $20 an hour upwards. The person I use has been known to read text onto an audio tape and doublecheck while playing it back. Other proofreaders begin at the last word and read backwards to ensure the story doesn't distract them!

Provide all of your proofreaders with the style sheet you have devised, so there is no confusion. If you are going to use a commercial printer who will supply you with galleys for proofing, you should do your utmost to get every error out now in this earlier stage. Correcting mistakes at the galley stage is time consuming and expensive, so better to do it now.

Don't skip on your proofreading and don't do it yourself. You will find that you are reading what you expect to be on the page instead of what is really there. A book with lots of errors looks like an amateurish effort and the most beautiful cover and page design in the world won't disguise this.

7 Saving money and keeping quality

Once upon a time everyone who wanted a 'real' book went to a printer who used plates and an offset press. Today self-publishers have the opportunity to use the latest advances in technology to help them save money. This is particularly so in the area of actual printing.

The quality of photocopying has improved so much that we can produce splendid books just by using a photocopier and a stapler or glue. Laser printers can also be used to create small numbers of great looking books, or provide camera-ready pages. One of the best options now is to photocopy the inside pages and have the cover printed, then do the binding yourself. But where do you find cheap photocopying?

Not so long ago 'quick' printers started popping up like flowers, offering fast, low-cost, high-volume photocopying. Some offer binding services, some offer even more. Like any printer, you need to get quotes and compare quality. For one job of 2000 double-sided pages I found there was a $200 difference between the cheapest and dearest quote.

One quick printer I used started out providing clear, dark copies then when the quality deteriorated, I discovered he wasn't using my pasted-up pages. He was using photocopies of my masters so he could set the machine on automatic to save himself time and money. Needless to say, he lost a customer.

If photocopying is your chosen option, you need to:

- Get quotes and compare prices.
- Look at whether your 'wants' are provided for (e.g. special paper, binding).
- Make sure the quality is the best possible.
- Provide clear, clean artwork.

You may find that these quick printers are too expensive for you. Try asking at your local community centre or neighbourhood house. They are often very supportive of self-publishers and you may be able to do a deal for cheaper photocopying, especially if you supply the paper. However, they are usually poorly funded, so don't expect them to be able to subsidise you.

You should also ask around for other places which provide inexpensive photocopying for individuals; for instance, the Victorian Writers' Centre assists members by offering reasonably priced photocopying facilities.

If you decide to use the photocopied insides/printed cover method, don't expect your book to look exactly like a commercially published one. If your printer is amenable, he may be happy to guillotine your books for you when the glue has dried or you've stapled them. That final trim can make quite a difference. On the other hand, you may want to embellish the handmade look a little more by using textured or recycled paper, or individual decorative touches. I have even seen books with all the page edges deliberately ragged.

Another alternative is to find a printer who uses the latest technology, such as the Xerox Docutech. This machine is like a cross between a high quality laser photocopier and a computer. It can either scan and print from your hard copy or from your disk. The computerised part of it will also line up all your margins, put in page numbers, allow scanned photos to be placed where you want them, and the final layout can be kept on disk for easy reprinting. It can print covers on stock up to 200gsm using scanned illustrations or photos. It's also very cost effective. It's major limitation at present is that it only prints in black, but there will be a colour version out by 2000 — I can't wait! It works with Postscript (PDF) files but there are programs such as Acrobat which will convert word-processing files for you. Not many printers have Docutechs, but it is worth searching out the ones who have, and they will job out your colour cover if they are no longer using an offset press as well.

At the other end of the spectrum, the craft aspect of creating books is coming back into fashion. While you can attend a variety of courses on how to make hard-case covers and your own paper and learn methods of hand binding, you can also learn this from library books, just as I did. It's worth finding out where your local binding and papermaking group operates. In Melbourne, Papermakers of Victoria Inc. meets at the Meat Market Craft Centre in North Melbourne and often holds exhibitions there. It's a great way to get ideas. People from all over Australia and New Zealand can become members of Papermakers and receive their newsletter. Write to Papermakers of Victoria, 14 Dalmor Avenue, Mitcham Vic 3132.

That's another important aspect of being a self-publisher — investigating what other people have done and how they accomplished it. Often it's by experimenting, or just because they were desperate. In one class I taught, a student, Margaret Campbell, found her book was going to be too thick for hand perfect binding just with glue. She got out her old Singer sewing machine at home, tested it on her paper and discovered she could sew her book in sections and glue the sections into the cover. Several other students also successfully used her method (and machine!). After I had shown another self-publisher how to perfect bind by hand using PVA glue, he experimented with his book and found a hot glue gun very effective, as long as he was quick about putting the pages in.

Generally you will find that anything less than 100 copies is quite manageable for one person to make. It's also financially to your advantage because small runs will cost you more if you print commercially. More than 100 copies may present a problem, although with your covers and insides already printed, you can make your books up as you require them after the initial selling period (i.e. at your leisure).

The only problem with making your book by hand is the time and labour involved. Some people just haven't got the time or can't be bothered with the necessary work. If this is you, then you have to look at other alternatives.

What if you are having your book commercially printed? How do you save money then? Firstly, before you go out to get your quotes, be aware of what is likely to cost you more money. Expensive elements include anything in full colour such as photographs, extra pages, the top quality paper and card or specialised stock, and 'fiddly bits' such as fold out pages. What will also be expensive is badly prepared artwork, especially where colour separations haven't been done properly. It's possible to inadvertently add hundreds of dollars to your printing costs, even if you use a professional, if instructions aren't clear or artwork is prepared the wrong way. Ask your printer for advice if you are in any doubt.

Keep quality in mind, even when you're trying to pare costs down. A book printed on paper which looks like newsprint will appear and feel cheap. Get a range of quotes and remember the cheapest may not be the best. A co-operative printer will help you keep costs down. Ask for your quotes to be broken down into the various components so you can see what is costing you extra money. Look at each component and see what can be reduced — could you use a less expensive cover stock, do without that embossing, have one less colour on your cover, use a gloss card stock instead of laminating? Can you reduce the number of pages, either by taking out pages or reducing type size or leading? Books printed on offset presses are often done in lots of eight pages, so if you have, for example, a 100-page book (12 x 8 pages plus 4 over), if you can reduce by four pages you will save the cost of a plate and a machine run.

You may also be tempted to save money by doing the imposition yourself, if your printer is not computerised. Imposition is pasting or placing pages on layout sheets in groups of four or eight (even up to 32) for plates to be made. Because books are often printed in sections and folded, the imposition won't be in numerical order, or even the same way up. Unless you've done lots of impositions and know how to work off a dummy, it's not something I'd recommend. Just one mistake and you could end

Saving money and keeping quality

up with a disaster. It's probably easier to leave it to the printer, who is used to doing it.

If you have done your sums, you have worked out the most economical way of printing and making your book and you know you will make a small profit, what do you do if you don't have the money you need? You can borrow it from a lending institution (not a good idea) or you can pre-sell your books before they are printed. Make your friends and family a special offer of some kind — hand-numbered and signed editions, an acknowledgement page, a discount price perhaps. Anything which will encourage them to give you the money up front.

This method of raising money is called advance subscription and is particularly useful for books such as family histories which have a ready-made audience. You can spread your net wider, depending on what kind of book you're publishing and its subject. Don't start your subscription drive until you are reasonably close to publication because, having handed over their money, your subscribers won't want to wait too long. Provide them with some information on the book, such as a sheet which gives the title, describes what the book is about, how big it will be, any special features. You could also give away a 'freebie' of some kind, for example, if your book is a collection of poetry, give subscribers one poem printed on nice paper as a subscriber's gift.

One advantage of pre-selling like this is it will soon show you how much of a salesperson you are (remember that question?). If you are unable to bring yourself to pre-sell, you won't do much better with the book in your hand.

Commercial printers often give you 30 days to pay your bill. If you have your launch within this time, and you have a spectacular launch and sell lots of copies, you could meet most of the bill from sales. However if you aren't too confident about this, you could ask friends and family to underwrite your book. This means they would give you a commitment in writing to lend you $100 or $200 if needed. If not needed, they pay nothing. It's better to spread it over quite a few people rather than owe one or two. You give each lender a free copy of the book instead of paying interest. Of course you must pay these loans back as soon as you can, but this is a great incentive to work out a good marketing plan.

By selling your books up front, you not only have the money for printing but you have your first guaranteed sales. It will help you finalise the number of books you will print and gauge the level of interest. Something for every self-publisher to consider!

8 The look of the book

It goes without saying that you want your book to look as good as possible. You don't want it to appear amateurish or cheap — you want it to be attractive yet subtly different or individual. These are some points for you to consider:

- What size is your book going to be? This will depend on its purpose — you may be producing a handy guide small enough for a pocket, or providing large, complex diagrams which need a bigger page size. Fiction and poetry books are generally smaller so people can carry them around easily in their bags to read on trains, trams and aeroplanes (hence the 'airport novel' which is a small paperback, and generally a light, entertaining read).

The most common sizes (with minor variations in between) are:

- airport novel: 112mm × 178mm
- literary novel: 130mm × 197mm
- large format paperback (between hardback and small paperback): 152mm × 235mm
- poetry collection: 140mm × 210mm

Take some books off your shelf and measure them to compare size with purpose. Most books are portrait (i.e. taller than they are wide). Landscape (wider than tall) books are likely to have a large number of photos in them, such as 'coffee table' books, or be recipe or technical books. If you find odd-sized books, try to work out the reason why they have been printed that way.

- Will its design style and production method suit the type of book it is? If it's a family cookbook, you could print it on recycled textured paper to give that aged feel. Will your method of binding suit the type of book it is? A cookbook or a how-to book usually needs to be able to open flat for easy reference while cooking or working. Therefore you may find spiral binding better than perfect binding. If it's a collection of poetry, you could include drawings or photos but don't make it look flowery and sentimental if that's not what your poetry is like.
- Where will your book be sold? If you are planning to put it in bookshops or sell to libraries, you need that spine with title and author clearly printed on it so it won't get lost on the shelves. If you're not selling, consider how it might be stored.
- How will it be read? As I mentioned, people like cookbooks and how-to books that lie flat while they're working. Small children like picture books that open right out. Elderly readers appreciate larger typefaces for easy reading.
- What are the important design elements you want to incorporate? The main advice is 'Keep It Simple'. Don't add what I call 'doo-dads' everywhere to pretty it up. Look at what other designers have done, what works and what doesn't. Clutter doesn't — white space does. You are trying to find that nice balance between consistency and experimenting. Once you have decided on the design of your pages, stick to it all the way through.

Some examples of simple, effective design elements I have seen include: a tiny leaf next to each page number; an anthology where the poets' names were in italics running down the side of each page; and a thin vertical line running from the title down to the third line of each poem (which linked title and poem in a visual cue).

Some design disasters include pages of an anthology with title, author and category of story in huge bold letters all around the text (it looked very heavy and messy), red printing on orange paper, and a collection of poems where the line spacings were different for each poem.

How can you be your own designer if you've never done it before? Firstly, by looking critically at what others have designed, the effect and the elements which create it. Decide what you like, what you think works (and what works is often not noticed at first glance, but mistakes certainly are). Secondly, remember the Keep It Simple rule and use it as your primary guideline. When your decisions have been made, or if you're not sure about how it will look, print out a few pages and ask friends and family for their opinions.

In terms of keeping it simple, here are some basic guidelines to help you:

- Leave decent margins all around, especially if your book will be perfect bound and trimmed later.
- Unless you have a good reason not to, justify your text on both the left and right margins. If you're using columns, try not to make them too narrow as you will end up with a lot of hyphenated words.
- Don't make your headings too large or fancy.
- Try to use only one typeface in the text and vary it with bold or italics if necessary.
- Don't use script typefaces even for headings.
- Think about your readers and make your text easy to read.

I recently assisted with a family history which was printed on A4 in order to accommodate all the photos. However, an A4 page filled with text would have been too tedious to read, and splitting the text into two columns made it look too much like a magazine. Also because many of the readers would be elderly, we decided to use 12 pt New Century Schoolbook for clarity. We eventually decided on one wide column of text down the middle of the page. Although this did mean more pages overall, it provided excellent readability, plenty of white space and looked very effective.

Some other points include:

- Start each chapter on a new page.

- Use the same typeface as in the text for front and end matter; use the same typeface for the title on both the cover and title page (for consistency).
- Don't change the leading of the text (space between lines) — keep it the same throughout the whole book.
- Don't double space between paragraphs — use indents instead as it saves space and avoids confusion, especially where there is dialogue or quotes.
- Enlarge your photos or illustrations to fill the whole page (or reduce to make more room) rather than cramming a couple of lines of text in the gap. Alternatively, you could leave the space empty.

To keep track of all your design decisions, either write out a style sheet or draw a simple diagram of your page, or both. On your design sheet you should include:

- page size and measurements for all margins, especially the inside gutter which is affected by binding
- typefaces and sizes selected for text, headings, subheadings, headers/footers, page numbers. The placement of headings, subheadings, headers/footers and page numbers — left, right or centre
- typeface and size for captions and location — left, right or centre
- positioning of illustrative material
- widows and orphans (i.e. you shouldn't start a page of text with only one line on it, nor end a page with the first line of a paragraph). Also avoid hyphenating a word over a page break.

If you are typesetting your book on a computer, the 'house design' style sheet provided below will be a handy checklist. If you're using a professional typesetter, it will act as a set of instructions and may be further extended. (See 8.1 on page 64 as an example.)

Typefaces (Fonts)

We read at least a dozen different typefaces every day, just in

The look of the book

the newspaper alone. You will find large blocks of text are usually in a serif typeface, such as Times Roman, and often advertising slogans or headings are sans serif. Serifs are the crosslines at the ends of letters. Large amounts of sans serif are hard to read but it's effective in short bursts. It is also often used for children's picture books and early readers because it looks more like their own printed handwriting.

Here are some samples to show you the differences:

This is a serif typeface (New Century Schoolbook 12pt).

This is a sans serif typeface (Arial 12 pt).

This is a script typeface (Brush Script MT 14 pt).

This is an ornate typeface (Zapf Chancery 12 pt).

There are many different typefaces — you really are best to stick to a readable serif typeface for your text, even poetry. I have seen poems in script and they are very hard on the eyes. I would even suggest avoiding script for titles. Again, look at what other people have done and analyse what looks most effective and, more importantly what is most *readable*.

Another aspect of typefaces is their size, which is measured in points. One point is equal to 0.0138 inches (.35mm), with 72 points to an inch. But you will find that 12 point Times will not necessarily be the same height and width as 12 point Helvetica. Don't go below 9 point for anything if you can avoid it, apart from captions perhaps, because it is too hard to read. For blocks of text, 11 point is very suitable, and up to 14 or 16 point for headings. You can use italics and bold for headings in the same typeface to create variety. As an example:

<small>This is 9 point Times.</small>

This is 12 point Times.

This is 12 point Times Italic.

This is 14 point Times bold.

I recommend that you actually take a block of text or a longer poem from your book and experiment by printing it out in different sizes and combinations of typefaces to see the effect.

You may have a computer program which also allows you to adjust the leading, which is the spacing between lines of text. A smaller typeface can be given a slightly bigger leading to make it more readable. Many computer programs set leadings automatically — the bigger word processing and desktop publishing programs allow you to alter it a point at a time.

> This is 10 point Times on an 11 point leading which is stipulated as 10/11. This is 10 point Times on an 11 point leading which is stipulated as 10/11. This is 10 point Times on an 11 point leading which is stipulated as 10/11. This is 10 point Times on an 11 point leading which is stipulated as 10/11.

> This is 10 point Times on a 12 point leading which is stipulated as 10/12. This is 10 point Times on a 12 point leading which is stipulated as 10/12. This is 10 point Times on a 12 point leading which is stipulated as 10/12. This is 10 point Times on a 12 point leading which is stipulated as 10/12.

> This is 10 point Times on a 14 point leading which is stipulated as 10/14. This is 10 point Times on a 14 point leading which is stipulated as 10/14. This is 10 point Times on a 14 point leading which is stipulated as 10/14. This is 10 point Times on a 14 point leading which is stipulated as 10/14.

Kerning is being able to squeeze individual letters closer together or spread them apart. It can be used for effect in headings or to save space, especially in narrow columns. Again, not all programs allow you to do it.

KERNING LETTERS CLOSER
KERNING LETTERS APART

If you are using columns of text in your book, be aware that larger typefaces may cause some very strange justification and gaps, as well as many hyphenated words. Reducing typeface size will help, and increasing the leading will assist readability.

The look of the book

Paper and card stock

There is a huge range of paper available these days, and most large cities have a paper oddments warehouse somewhere where the self-publisher can buy end-of-line or extra stock from paper suppliers. For those not so fortunate, there is still a small range of coloured and textured papers stocked by office suppliers. Just be careful of cost, as I have seen 100 sheets of parchment selling for over $22.

Paper now can be coated or uncoated, plain or textured or recycled, gloss or matt, and card stock is the same. If you ask to see a commercial printer's paper sample catalogues, you will often be faced with a choice of several hundred different kinds, so it helps enormously to know first what you are looking for.

The weight of paper is measured in grams per square metre, so you will hear photocopy paper, for example, referred to as 80gsm and card may be 140gsm up to 280gsm or even 400gsm. Very thin paper is often used to save money, but the problem is that the printing shows through on the other side. 80gsm is really the lightest weight you should use. The strength of the paper is also a factor as some fold better than others. A paper which can't withstand constant folding is no good for dust jackets or fold out maps.

Paper also has a direction of grain (like wood) and this is especially important in hand-made or hand-bound books. It is much harder to fold against the grain and the fold often doesn't sit straight. Try folding a sample of your chosen card and paper in two different directions to see which way the grain lies.

Whiteness is another factor. While you might choose a flecked or off-white recycled paper for effect, you don't want a paper that looks like newsprint. The acidity of your paper will affect its life as well as the life of anything mounted or in contact with it. You can now buy archival paper which will last 500 years.

Plain paper is available in either A4 (210mm x 297mm) or A3 (297mm x 420mm) in reams of 500 sheets. (Please note that in Australia and New Zealand these are now the standard sizes — quarto and foolscap are no longer in use.) Commercial printers buy their paper in much larger sheets, usually A0 (841mm x

1189mm) and cut it down to the size they need, trying to get as little wastage as possible. This is why an odd sized book will cost you more, because it will be cut from sheets this size and you will pay for wastage as well.

Always check the availability of your selected stock, as well as its cost and whether it suits your printing method. Some textured papers and cards cannot be photocopied as the toner won't bond properly. Many photocopiers can't handle heavier cards. Some cards don't like large areas of ink and will still smudge weeks later, unless you have them laminated which will cost more. Be careful also about using heavier weights of paper in perfect binding. The larger the book, the more likely it is that heavier paper might come away from the binding, so you would have to use burst binding instead of perfect, or reduce your paper weight.

Ink

In most cases you will be using black ink for your text, either by photocopying or printing. There are very few books which look effective printed in coloured ink as it affects readability.

If you are using a commercial printer, you will be more concerned with ink colour when it comes to your cover. The range of colours is even wider than the range of paper, with dozens of shades of every colour of the rainbow. If you have a particular colour in mind, ask to see the printer's ink swatches and match it exactly. (This is the Pantone Matching System.) The code number tells him the mix of colours to create your exact shade. (See Chapter 10 for more detail on colour and separations.)

Binding

There is a range of bindings available, and each method has advantages and disadvantages.

- Saddle stitched — this is the simplest method, two or three staples through the spine. The advantage is that it's cheap and you can easily do it yourself with a long stapler. The main disadvantage is these books get lost on the shelf because they

The look of the book

have no spine. Also people tend to think they don't look like 'real' books, but if you're not selling through bookshops this may not be an issue. Saddle stitching is great for smaller books but the more pages you have, the more likely you are to get 'creep', which is the right-hand edges fanning out. Trimming with an industrial guillotine will fix this (you could ask a friendly printer to do it for you or pay for the service).

- Comb or spiral binding — these require a machine to punch holes in the paper and thread the comb or spiral through. The advantage is that your book will lie flat when open, which for some books is a must. Disadvantages include the appearance (comb bindings tend to look like manuals or handbooks so it's not recommended for fiction or poetry) and there is no spine for the title and author to be printed on. Metal or plastic-coated spiral binding can be quite expensive. I have been quoted $3 per book!
- Perfect binding — this is usually done by a machine which roughens the spine edge of the paper to take the glue better, then folds the cover around the pages. The glue dries very quickly. Advantages include the ability to print author and title on the spine, it looks attractive, and it is what most readers have come to expect, rightly or wrongly, so it's competitive in the marketplace. It's usually a fairly strong binding for an average-sized book. The disadvantages are that it is more expensive, especially in small print runs (e.g. perfect binding can cost $1 per copy for 100 copies but 50c per copy for 300 copies), and can fall apart if treated roughly or heavier paper is used. It is difficult to perfect bind books with less than 60 to 70 pages (less than 5mm thick) because the machine has trouble handling them. Perfect bound books will not open flat, unless you force them to by creasing (and often breaking) the spine.

It is possible to perfect bind by hand, which is an excellent alternative for books with less than 60 pages. You can use hidden staples or sewing for extra strength. Doing it by hand is labour intensive but very economical. (See Appendix 1 for instructions.)

- Burst binding — this is like perfect binding but the pages are

not trimmed and roughed, they are left folded and notches cut out to allow the glue to go further in. It is stronger than perfect binding but more expensive, and your printing method has to be one where you end up with folded pages, not cut sheets.
- Section sewing — this is when 16, 32 or 64 page sections of a book are sewn with thread, then sewn together and bound. It's a method commonly used with hard cover books but more and more paperbacks are also using this method now, by sewing in sections then gluing into a soft cover. It is a much stronger binding, and also allows the book to open flat on a surface. Disadvantages are the cost and that not many printers and binders do it.

Hard or soft cover?

Although it sounds the most expensive option (and usually is), there may be very good reasons for your book being a hard cover edition. Family and local histories, in particular, are books which are expected to last a long time. Coffee-table books are also usually hard cover, as are many large recipe books. If you're not sure, ask your intending buyers what they would prefer, and if they would pay extra for a hard cover edition. The extra $10 or so may be worth it to them.

Most hard cover books have a casing of thick sturdy cardboard covered with fabric, with the pages sewn in sections then sewn and glued into the casing with endpapers. You will need to make sure your binder produces a satisfactorily tight finish, so the book doesn't fall apart or come away from the casing. Hard cover books usually have a dust jacket to wrap around which will both protect the book and provide the opportunity for colour and illustrations. It is also possible to have your books bound in leather, but as this is extremely expensive, you might want to have just one bound like this as an heirloom.

Another alternative is a soft cover of plain white card, a stapled or perfect bound spine, with a dust jacket wrapped around it. It gives the book a quality hard cover appearance without the cost of that binding. It is also possible to have a soft cover with

The look of the book

extended flaps which fold inside like a dust jacket (called a gatefold cover).

The cover

If you are selling your books, your cover is your most important marketing tool. It has to be the best you can afford. The first thing a buyer does is look at the cover; if it appeals, they pick it up and turn it over to read the back, which is where your blurb is printed.

Visit your nearest bookshop and check out a range of covers. Which ones catch your eye? What seems to be the current trend? Covers with boxed pictures are about five years out of date. At the moment the fashion is a picture which fills the whole cover (often the back as well) with printing over the top. Look at the back of the title page when you find designs you like. Often the cover designer's name is here. Search out the work of someone like Mary Callahan who is very popular with publishers and has designed some beautiful covers (e.g. Robert Dessaix's *Night Letters* and Drusilla Modjeska's *The Orchard*).

What are the elements which make up an eye-catching or effective cover design? Is it just the illustration or photo chosen, or is it the way it is used, the colour contrasts, the placement of title and author? Where does balance come in?

When you have decided on the elements of your cover design, make up a dummy, as close as you can get to what it will finally look like. You can use your computer, or cut and paste with coloured pens and paints. Move things around to gauge the different effects. Then ask yourself these questions:

- Does your cover design effectively convey what kind of book you have written? Does it make the book 'pick-uppable' and inviting? Have you used colour and card stock to the best advantage? Have you tried out all your ideas? Have you looked at other options such as a dust jacket, fold out flaps, gluing items on individually and hand colouring/lettering (for small print runs)?
- If you have decided to use a professional designer, have you given the person an accurate brief or some examples of what

Figure 8.1 Typesetting specification sheet

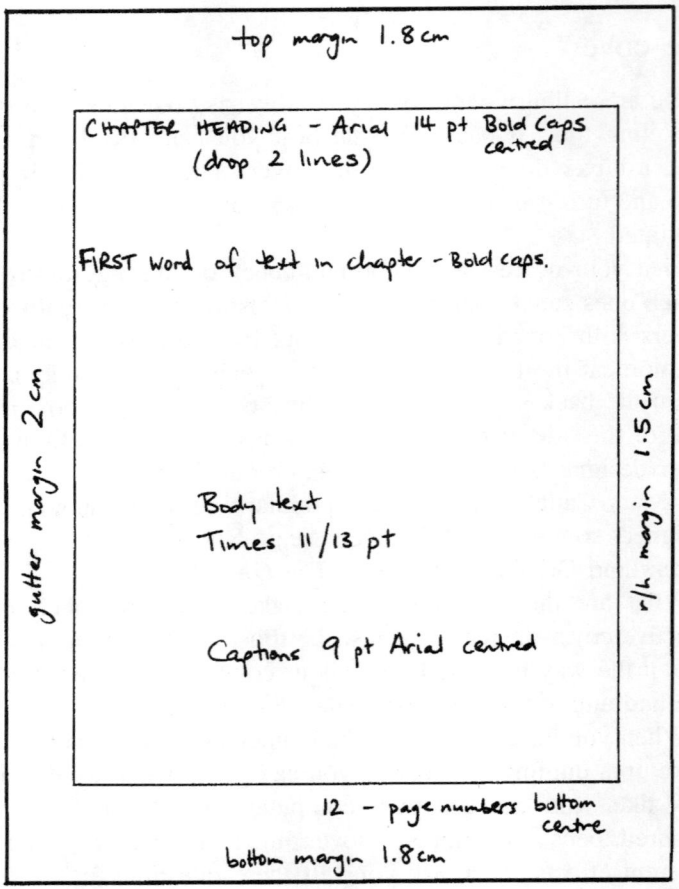

you want? Have you seen other covers this person has done? Some designers have a particular style from which they find it difficult to deviate. Others don't understand the financial limitations of self-publishers. Some don't even understand the printing process and can't prepare material properly. One person I know paid for a designer who did such a poor job of the colour separations that the printer had to redo them and it doubled the price of the printing. Ask to see other work and

The look of the book

ask how the final artwork will be prepared. Check with your printers that this artwork is suitable for them to be able to make their plates simply and efficiently.
- Have you allowed for a spine, if you are having one? Perfect binding requires the width of the spine plus a little extra for the scoring and folding. Test your dummy cover on the number of pages you will have.

Some books you may find very useful if you want to know more about these aspects of design, as well as detailed information about printing processes, are *Pocket Pal* published by Associated Pulp and Paper Mills (many printers keep one handy), *Editing for Print* by Geoffrey Rogers (Writer's Digest Books, Ohio, USA), *The Illustrated Handbook of Desktop Publishing and Typesetting* by M.L. Kleper (Windcrest Books, USA) and *Bookmaking* by Marshall Lee (R.R. Bowker, New York). More information on covers is in Chapter 11.

9 Limitations and problems

As a self-publisher, you will inevitably find there are limitations to what you can produce, simply because of time and/or money. Your aim should be to work inside these limitations to the best of your ability. On the other hand, many problems can be solved if you have allowed yourself plenty of time. Mistakes and disasters usually occur when your launch date is looming and you make panic decisions.

A lack of time means you may decide to pay for work you could do yourself, such as the typesetting or photocopying. Time does mean money and I would suggest you do your sums regarding the bits you'd have to pay others to do, then obtain quotes from several of the various companies around which offer to publish for you, such as Fast Books in Sydney or PenFolk in Melbourne (there are quite a few now). In New Zealand a number of printers (such as The Caxton Press and Craig Printing Co Ltd) undertake publishing on behalf of self-publishers. Unit costs are quite high because they do everything for you. For most self-publishers, doing it all themselves saves money and ensures a reasonable profit margin. However if time is your limitation, or there is no way you can get access to the necessary technology, one of these companies may be an option. You still need to get quotes, compare prices, services and quality.

On the other hand, if money is your limiting factor, you will bypass them altogether and look at the most economical ways

Limitations and problems

of making your book yourself. Hints on saving money are covered in Chapter 7, but this whole book is aimed at how to do it yourself, so read on!

Other limitations are more to do with your actual book. If you are photocopying, you will be limited to the size of photocopy paper (A4 or A5) unless you have access to a proper industrial guillotine. Even if you are using a commercial printer, it's best not to stray too far outside traditional paper sizes because the printer works from a traditional size and is limited to what can be cut out of it (a bit like trying to cut a garment from a length of cloth).

Depending on your printing method, you may be limited by multiples of pages, e.g. if your book is A5 and you are photocopying onto A4, you will be working in multiples of four pages at a time. If your book is being printed, you may find you will be working in multiples of eight. Make sure you know these page parameters, otherwise you may end up having to print an extra sheet of four or eight with only one page on it (so you have to pay for an extra plate and paper).

There are ways around this problem — maybe fewer preliminary pages or one less illustration or photo. If there is no leeway there, you could look at reducing your typeface slightly, expanding your margins slightly or reducing your leading. If none of these are possible, rather than end up with blank pages at the end, look at how to fill them constructively. Add a couple of photos or illustrations, add an order form for further copies of the book, put in a special acknowledgements page — whatever suits your book.

What if you are going to have problems because you don't own and can't afford a high-quality laser printer for camera-ready artwork? One option is to only use a commercial printer who can produce your book from your disk. Then your printout can serve as a guide for layout and proofing. If you are photocopying your book and need your printed pages to be 600dpi or laser quality, there are places where you can take your disk and get it printed out. Some possibilities include your local library, friends, local tertiary institutions, community-based training centres and small businesses who deal in graphic arts or desktop publishing. Of course you will have to pay for this service (unless your friend is very generous) and the cost ranges from fifty cents to a dollar per page. Make sure that your computer system and program is compatible with theirs, and print out some sample pages first to check that nothing has been altered, such as headings, fonts, page breaks, etc.

Another problem which can arise is a permission for use of a quote or excerpt not arriving. If you've kept an eye on your list, you'll know who's being tardy in replying. Don't wait — follow up as soon as you suspect there's some delay. If you're at the final stage of proofing and are nearly ready to print but the permission has not arrived, you need to make a decision. Will you postpone everything while you wait a bit longer, or will you leave that quote out? It depends on your progress in obtaining it, but unless you're very sure it's going to turn up when promised, you may have to delete it from your book. Only you can make that decision.

Sometimes the things which become the stuff of nightmares are the little extras which were planned to add that original touch — a fold-out map or family tree at the back, a special page of mounted colour photos in the middle, a hand-painted cover. The basic remedy is time and patience. In small print runs, when you have the ability to cope with this extra work or financial outlay, these elements will remain finicky and tedious. In larger print runs, they may be far more trouble than they are worth. Be very realistic about their value in your overall production, and very realistic about the headaches they might cause you.

At some point in your publishing venture, you will start to wonder why on earth you ever attempted the whole darn thing. It seems to be the stupidest idea you've ever come up with and not worth the trouble. Don't worry, you're not alone. Very few people sail through the entire process without a hitch or a qualm. At some point you'll probably curse the day the computer was ever invented, if nothing else! If you are feeling overwhelmed and depressed, take some time to sit down and remind yourself of why you're doing it, what your goals are and how you'll feel when the book is there in your hands. Refer back to the first questions in this book, review your progress along the timeline

Limitations and problems

and decide if you will be able to meet your launch deadline without distress, panic and a nervous breakdown. If the reason for your stress is that you are running out of time, move your launch date forward and give yourself plenty of room to manoeuvre, to get all those details right, and to produce the kind of book you dreamed of, the one you'll be proud and happy to show around and sell.

10 What else apart from the text?

There are a number of other 'bits' which your book will need, and once you have tackled the body of the text you can look at what else is required. It's a good idea to make a list of what will go between the covers and the order in which it will appear. This running order sheet will help you work out what will be on your right (recto) and left (verso) pages. Preliminary pages are often numbered with Roman numerals (e.g. i–xii), then comes the body of the text, then end matter which is included in the general paging. You could also include a list of illustrations and the pages on which they will appear.

The following list of elements covers both fiction and non-fiction books, so you should include only what is relevant. Novels, for example, rarely have a contents page these days. If in doubt, look at several examples of published books in your field and see what they have in them.

Front matter

Half-title page — This is the first right-hand page when you open the book. Traditionally it held only the title of the book in a smaller typeface. These days it can hold the blurb, the author's biographical note, a short excerpt or 'taster' from the book, or it may be deleted altogether. The back of the half title page is often blank, or sometimes used to list the author's previous titles.

What else apart from the text?

Title page — This carries the title (and sub-title if there is one) in the same typeface as the cover, the author's name, and often the publisher's name and logo. If you aren't publishing under a trading name, don't put your own name in again. Sometimes the year of publication appears on the title page — again, I wouldn't recommend this as it dates the book too quickly and obviously.

Back of the title page (Imprint page) — This is where all your publishing information belongs, including copyright notice and year of publication and statement of rights, publisher's name and address (yours — handy for future orders), ISBN, printer's details, cataloguing information if you have it, and other information which may be relevant, such as the cover designer's name.

Note: The half-title page, title page and back of title page are not numbered.

Contents — Usually used in non-fiction books or collections and anthologies. It will depend on your book. Make sure your page numbers are accurate — it's one of the last things you need to triple-check in proofreading.

List of photographs/illustrations — Most books don't bother these days, but if you want your readers to be able to find particular diagrams or photos easily, this list with page numbers will be helpful.

Dedication — If you want to dedicate your book to someone this should go on a page by itself.

Acknowledgements — You may want to thank people for their assistance, either with publishing or research perhaps. You may also need to acknowledge permissions, quotes, previously published work, etc. The acknowledgements can go at the beginning of the book or the end.

Foreword — This is usually written by someone else who talks about your book. It's an advantage to get someone famous or highly respected in your field as it helps to sell the book, and their name should appear on the cover. It's not mandatory, especially in fiction and poetry.

Preface/Introduction — This is usually written by the author. An introduction should add something relevant or important to the book, so if in doubt, leave it out.

End matter

Appendices — It's preferable to use appendices to list extra relevant information, rather than clutter your text. Number your appendices from 1 upwards so you can refer to them clearly in the text.

Glossary — This usually provides explanations of terms not easily understood by the reader, or tables such as metric conversions or currencies. (Tables can also appear in the appendices.)

Footnotes — These are generally only necessary when a large number of references are cited in the text. Some books list footnotes at the end of each chapter, others put them all at the end under chapter numbers.

Bibliography — This is a list of books used as references during research, or further recommended reading.

Note: Footnotes and bibliographies can be set out in several different ways. Choose one style, such as the Harvard style, and stick to it. When referring to material from the Public Record Office, use their entry method with appropriate punctuation e.g. Victorian Public Record Office, VPRS 520 Unit 1 Item 4.

Index — Any non-fiction book should have an index, if you can manage one. It is usually prepared last when you have all your page numbers available in typesetting as they will be printed. An index includes people, places and topics, and is arranged with headings and sub-headings in alphabetical order, with references to page numbers. If you are unfamiliar with how to prepare an index, you can refer to a simple guide in the *Style Manual* (Australian Government Publishing Service) or use a text designed specifically for the task such as *Indexing from A to Z* by Hans Wellisch (H.W. Wilson Company, New York, 1991), *Indexing Books* by Nancy Mulvaney (University of Chicago Press, 1994), and *Indexing, the art of* by Norman Knight (Allen & Unwin, London, 1979). Most references recommend a compilation on file cards or uniform pieces of paper, arranged alphabetically and typed up when finished.

You can also use the indexing function on your word processing program. Both Word and Wordperfect (later versions) provide indexing capabilities, and will automatically provide page numbers for the same index reference word throughout your document if you create a concordance file for it. As with the spelling check function though, you still need to double-check all entries yourself to ensure no errors or omissions.

Other elements of your book

Illustrations — The easiest to work with are clear, black ink line drawings because they reproduce so well in any printing process. As you are not allowed to use other people's art without permission, you may have an artist friend you can call on, or you could provide your own as long as they will add to your book and not detract. There are books of copyright-free illustrations available, or computer-generated pictures — be very careful about using these as they are usually recognisable and look 'ordinary'.

If you are using art which is shaded or coloured in some way, you may need to have it screened or bromided. Because, like photographs, these kinds of illustrations are made up of a number of areas of varying light and dark, they need to be broken down into dots to reproduce this shading. This is done by using a screen which can be between 65 and 130 dots per square inch. Look at some examples around your home — newspaper photographs are usually around 65 to 80, fine colour work may be from 110 to 130. (Use a magnifying glass to see the difference.)

Therefore a light area of shading will have dots further apart and a dark area will have dots closer together. Most commercial printers have bromiding facilities, or art houses can provide this service. The cost will be from $15 upwards per photo or illustration, often more. The same principle applies to colour photos and artwork, but is more complex, involving colour combinations and registers. Refer to the *Style Guide* or similar for detailed explanations and examples of how colours are overlaid.

If you are photocopying your book but have one or more black and white photos you want to use, you will find they will not photocopy well. However if you have them bromided (screened) you can use these instead which will give you a much better quality of reproduction. Beware of plastic screens sold for use with photocopiers — they don't work very well.

If you want your shaded illustration screened, try one first to see what result you get. You may find it disappointing as this process can often take all the 'texture' or life out of a picture. It is also expensive if you have to screen everything. This kind of art can also be scanned into a computer, but again, check the result first.

Don't be tempted to provide a fancy border or even just a box frame for everything. Let the picture stand on its own first. Don't give into the temptation to fill every white space with a picture or doo-dad of some kind — less is more.

Photographs — Your photographs can be bromided (as explained above) or they can be computer scanned, depending on your commercial printer's equipment (or your own). In either case, you don't need the negative and the original photo will not be harmed in any way, which is great for precious ancient family photos. Scanning will not always give you a high quality reproduction but it is cheaper and easier — it often depends on the quality of the laser printer and software.

Photos can always be cropped or enlarged to suit your page size or layout. The best way to provide your printer with specific instructions on this is to photocopy your photo and either enlarge or reduce it to your desired size as an example, or draw on the photocopy to indicate cropping area. I also recommend placing each photo with all relevant instructions, including which page it is to appear on, into a separate plastic envelope.

Don't use poor quality photos which are too dark or damaged

What else apart from the text?

as none of these processes will make them look any better and they will often come out worse. Professional restoration work is available if the photo is important to you, but should be done first. If you are taking photos for your book, use a good quality black and white film. Colour photos will reproduce well in black and white as long as there is enough dark and light contrast in them.

If you are using reprints of original photos and hand mounting them in your books, look around for cheap rates for multiple copies. I have been able to obtain 200 reprints for 40 cents each, less than half the usual cost. Use the appropriate spray adhesive for mounting as many glues will wrinkle the paper and damage the photo. It is also possible to have colour photocopies made of your colour illustrations, even watercolours, and either hand mount or insert them as extra pages. Again, get quotes from a range of services as prices vary considerably and you should get a discount for quantity.

You can usually gain permission to use photos from library collections such as the La Trobe Library at the State Library of Victoria, or the Alexander Turnbull Library in the National Library, Wellington. The request to use should be made in writing, as with any permission, and they will provide the correct wording for acknowledgement.

Captions — Most photos and some illustrations will need captions. These can be typeset with the text on the relevant pages, or typeset separately and cut and pasted on afterwards. Captions are part of your page design so choose a complementing typeface (a small sans serif can look effective) and centre your caption where possible. Captions in odd places may also need to be typeset separately and pasted on, or scanned if your commercial printer is working off a disk. If in doubt, ask the printer.

Captions should add information or enlighten, so subjects' full names are needed as well as place, date and, if possible, the photographer's name. If it's a newspaper photo or one from a library collection, acknowledgement should be in the caption, e.g. 'Reproduced by courtesy of the Daily Blah'. Further information can be included on your acknowledgements page.

Maps — These are copyrighted, like most material not created by you, and permission is required. Keep in mind what will happen to a colour map which is reproduced in black and white (and the cost of colour reproduction).

You can draw your own maps, on your computer, or by using a good quality black ink pen on white paper. Lettering can be done by hand, or on the computer and pasted on. As this can be very finicky, try creating a larger map and then reducing it by photocopying. However, be careful that you don't lose all your detail. This also applies if you are reducing large maps you have permission to use. It's better just to reproduce the section you want. A large map which unfolds from inside the back cover may be an option, but these can be costly and difficult to mount effectively (there's nothing like a map which won't refold the way it opened!)

If you want your map to look 'aged', for a family history perhaps, you could use simple calligraphy for your lettering, and print or photocopy it onto parchment-type paper.

Family trees, other charts and diagrams — Again, you can draw these by hand or create them on the computer if you know how. Sans serif typefaces take up less room and are easier to read in smaller sizes.

Original documents — These can include birth, death and marriage certificates, letters, diaries, indenture papers, newspaper cuttings, postcards, advertisements and greeting cards. Where relevant, make sure you check about permission to use. You will need originals of a reasonable quality and these can be scanned, bromided or photocopied. Many of these documents have no borders and will get lost on the page when reproduced, so you may need to place them within a box or frame, but keep it simple. Use these kinds of documents with care, making sure they are adding to your book, not cluttering it up.

If there is anything at all in your book which requires more than one colour, you need to take into account the added cost and the method required to reproduce. Get quotes and advice

What else apart from the text?

and then decide if it's worth it, or if the material can be effectively reproduced in black and white.

It's one of the advantages of a small print run that there are many individual touches which you can add to make your books very special. Just remember the 'Keep It Simple' principle.

11 The cover

The cover of your book has several important jobs to do, and that doesn't include holding the pages together. It has to make the book look attractive and 'pick-uppable', it has to contain important information such as the title, author and blurb, and it has to represent and, to some extent, interpret what is contained inside. Even many commercially published books only achieve limited success with their covers.

The challenge for you as a self-publisher is to aim for the best cover possible with the resources available to you, which often comes down to a combination of money and imagination. Spend as much as you can afford on your cover. These days you cannot underestimate its importance. Be aware of trends — at the moment the fashion is to have the illustration or photo fill the whole cover and print the title and author's name over the top. Boxed or framed pictures can make the book look dated. The cover is the place where you can experiment and be daring, as long as you don't end up with a regurgitated pizza effect! Look at lots of other covers and think about what effect you want to create — a sense of fun, history, elegance, or ultra-modern?

Some cover disasters I have seen include ink colours too light or dark for the card stock colour with the result that the words and illustrations were illegible, brown ink on a beige card (looked like a timber catalogue), a photo printed on textured card so all the depth was lost, badly bromided photos that gave the appear-

The cover

ance of a cheap tabloid newspaper, very bad hand-drawn pictures and dot matrix lettering. And these are just a few, all of which could have been easily fixed.

Some innovative and successful covers have included hand-mounted colour photos (which were sealed by laminating), full colour covers printed on a colour bubblejet printer (which unfortunately wrecked the printer but looked great!), and a drawing of a bird in flight which spread over the whole cover. The last example was originally going to be printed on marbled card — luckily the author ran off a sample first and discovered the marble pattern made the bird look as if it had some terrible disease, so she was able to change her stock in time.

If you are having your cover printed, perhaps to go with photocopied insides, prepare your artwork very carefully. You should measure and allow for the spine, including extra for folding around, and you may need to allow for trimming after the book has been assembled. Seek advice and/or quotes on any colour photograph separations or other special work needed. The use of more than one colour of ink will also require separations, i.e. whatever is to be printed in each colour will require a plate of its own and therefore artwork of its own. When these are laid over each other (and printed over each other) they will come together to create the final effect. You will need to make sure everything lines up exactly (registers), and the best way to prepare this material is to use a light table (a glass topped table with a light source underneath so you can see through several layers of paper at once). You should also decide where to place your blurb and other back cover material, as well as what goes on the front and spine.

Because the printing process with colours is more complicated and expensive, especially in the plates and machine setup, it's often advisable to have more covers printed than you immediately need. Then it's a simple process later to have a few more insides printed without the setup expenses of the cover again. Extra covers can also be used on their own for publicity and displays. Everyone would love to have a full colour cover, using a spectacular photo or illustration of some kind, but for many people it's just not feasible. You should look at what's possible with just two colours and a coloured card stock, and use a combination of imagination and simplicity. I have seen some great covers using black and white photos but printing them in shades of blue or green.

Another option, especially if you can't afford perfect binding but want a quality effect, is to have a plain stapled book with a lovely dust jacket. There are some high quality, thicker, gloss and matte art papers now which make hard-wearing dust jackets. There is also the possibility of extending to fold-out flaps, similar to a dust jacket but actually part of the cover. (Remember these options will have no spine.)

If you are producing a small number of books, especially if they are intended as gifts, you can be as creative as you like. Handmade paper and card, hand-painted or individual illustrations, special hand-crafted bindings, hand-mounted pictures and photos — the scope is endless. If you do want to sell these books, you will probably never recoup the cost of your labour but they are very satisfying and everyone will love them. If you create individually designed and decorated covers, don't be surprised if you are asked for more of this one or that one.

The range of card available for covers is enormous, especially since the papermaking industry moved into recycled, textured and flecked stock. Your commercial printer should have lots of samples for you to look at. If you are making your own covers, search for a paper warehouse near you which stocks oddments and off-cuts. Try the Yellow Pages and ring first to check exactly what is available, as many paper suppliers have only standard lines. It'll usually be potluck what you get, but if you find something you like, buy as much as you can afford. You may never see it again.

Generally cover stock should be at least 175gsm in weight, so it will be sturdy and wear well. If you are photocopying your cover, keep in mind that many photocopiers won't accept more than 140gsm card. If you are choosing a glossy card stock, check that it won't retain fingerprints and damp marks. Also check with the printer that any large areas of ink will dry properly, especially if you are using any reverse print.

Most commercially published books have laminated covers.

The cover

This is a thin layer of plastic coating over the card to protect it from marking. There are companies which specialise in laminating and it is possible to find one which will do a small run of 200 or less if you phone around. Don't confuse this process with the double-sided thicker laminating which many small copying businesses and libraries offer. Double-sided laminating is expensive, it is quite unyielding and the card is hard to fold and bind afterwards. It also tends to bow and not sit flat. On the other hand, if you are forced to use a thin card stock and are stapling, this laminating might be suitable for you as it will actually strengthen your covers. Hints for double-sided laminating — score and crease the card before applying the lamination. Then after assembling your books, place them between four layers of flat fabric, such as calico, and steam iron briskly to and fro. Place under heavy books while still hot to flatten.

What else goes on the cover?

An important part of the cover design is the typeface for the title, author's name and blurb. The typeface must suit the kind of book it is, be very readable and be the right size to balance with the illustration and the size of the book. It must also be readable in smaller sizes (your sub-title is not necessary on the spine). The title and author's name on the spine should read from left to right when the book is flat on the table, front cover up. If your foreword is written by someone well known or famous, place that person's name on the cover too.

Don't underestimate the importance of what goes on the back of the cover. I've heard many self-publishers say they don't need a blurb, yet it is your second most powerful selling tool after your cover. Watch people in a bookshop — they look at the cover first, then automatically pick a book up and turn it over to read what's on the back.

A great blurb is not an easy thing to write. You need to tempt the reader into looking further or buying the book with the expectation they are getting what you've promised. And you have to fulfil that expectation. Don't cheat and make your novel out to be steamy and sensual when it's a light romance, or infer your book is contemporary poetry when it's full of traditional rhyming verse.

A non-fiction blurb needs to inform potential readers about what they will find in your book, what it covers and how extensively. You are being informative here, not just enticing. Read lots of blurbs of all kinds to see how other people do it. Spend as much time as you need on writing your blurb and get feedback from plenty of people. Make it work for you, not against you.

You can also place nice quotes from reviews of your other books on the back of your cover (if you have any), or even nicer quotes from well-known people who have read the manuscript and commented favourably. Blurbs and quotes should be readable and well spaced out, not all crammed in together, and it's a good idea to use the same typeface as the body of the text.

If your book has a dust jacket or extended flaps, use them to provide extra material about your book. Your photo and biographical details should go on the back flap, as well as a list of your other publications. You can use the front flap for your blurb (which frees the back of the cover up for quotes and recommendations), or for extra enticing material about your book.

You don't have to put the price of your book on the back cover, and you probably shouldn't so that you're not tied to it in the future. But if you have got a barcode, you definitely need to place that there, usually at the bottom.

Remember when you are designing your cover to focus on impact, balance and making it 'pick-uppable'. Your design should look balanced both when it is spread open (so you can see front, back and spine all at once) and when it is closed and only the front is visible. Try to construct a mock-up of your cover, as close to the final printed version as possible, and try it out on people. Place it on a display among other books and look at it from a distance. What effect does it convey? Would you pick it up for a second look?

12 Methods of printing

Up until recently, the photocopier and laser printer were probably the most advantageous new technology for the self-publisher. Photocopying has improved in quality to the point where you can produce books that look good, don't cost the earth and are flexible in their production. Laser printers have enabled us to create camera-ready artwork for most printing processes. And of course with computers we are only limited by our expertise and software.

The following is a range of printing options currently available, including the newest technology and some future possibilities. If you live in the country, away from this range of services, consider making the trip to your nearest regional centre or city in order to investigate what is available at what cost. Your local commercial printer might be convenient, but if he's using an offset press and doesn't have the required equipment, he won't be able to keep costs down for you, especially on smaller print runs.

No matter which printing option you choose, if anyone is providing you with any services, clear communication about what you want is essential.

Offset printing

This is offered by most small and large commercial printers. The offset press works on a principle of ink transfer from plate to cylinder to paper. Plates can be paper or metal and will last for thousands of copies. Metal plates can be reused later, paper plates can't, so obviously metal ones are more expensive.

Offset printing fulfils a wide range of printing needs, from full colour to heavy card stock to ink colours of every shade and hue. It is the base cost of the plates which tends to make it expensive, i.e. no matter how many copies you want, you still have to pay the same amount for your plates. Thus you could be quoted $1000 for 200 copies and $1300 for 400 copies, enticing you into the larger print run. Once the machine is set up, the paper and ink costs are relatively less.

Larger offsets can print 32 or 64 pages at a time. Your average local printer is likely to use plates that will print four pages of A5 at a time, and then another four on the reverse. It is also likely that you will have to paste up those pages (or he will do it and charge you), a task which many people don't like to tackle.

Many smaller printers don't have perfect-binding machinery on their premises — they will 'job out' that part, which could work out more expensive. However they will collate, organise binding and trim your book. You need to check out exactly what services the printer can provide, the quality of his work (ask to see samples) and how he requires your artwork to be presented. If he is to complete any extra work for you, such as separations or paste-ups, ask for a separate costing for this.

Larger commercial printers sometimes specialise in full colour work and 'upmarket' publications, so their quote might be higher and their attitude to your job a little snooty. They also might not be interested in small print runs.

Quick printers

There are dozens of these, everywhere you look, especially in business areas. You may be familiar with franchise names such as Snap, KwikKopy and Pink Panther, and they are often called instant printers, or copy centres in New Zealand. Their main clients are companies who want quick printing of business cards, invoices, reports etc. They offer high speed photocopying, colour

Methods of printing

photocopying and basic binding. Most don't offer perfect binding and most don't have a very wide range of paper and card stock. Some offer double-sided laminating.

Be very careful in your use of these printers. Their quotes vary as widely as commercial printers, as does the quality of their work. There are lots of smaller ones around, as well as the big franchises, so look in the Yellow Pages and investigate a range of prices.

Book 'makers'

A new industry has sprung up in the past few years, led by Pat Woolley's FastBooks in Sydney. These companies offer every service to you which self-publishers usually organise themselves, from typing and proofing through to printing and binding. They virtually take your manuscript and present you with the required number of finished books a few weeks later. More expensive? You bet, because they're doing all the work.

Even if you want a simple book with a two-colour cover and nothing fancy, you will rarely pay much less for the finished product than you can sell it for. I have seen a range of basic prices and perused a few quotes and certainly, if you are not able to do all the work and organising yourself, these companies are a wonderful alternative. But there is no opportunity to cut costs and experiment when you hand it over to someone else.

If you are contemplating using one of these operations, ask to see a range of books they have done and get precise quotes, particularly when you want something a little (or a lot) different from the average. One advantage is that they will keep your book on disk so that reprints aren't too difficult. Also because they focus on books and are very experienced, they can help and advise you where necessary.

New technology

Imagine a high-speed, laser-quality photocopier combined with a computer which scans your text, either from hard copy or disk, scans and inserts your illustrations and photos, pops in page numbers and prints the whole thing in a couple of hours. It's a sight to behold, and it's solved all my little problems, from my hatred of paste-ups to my little laser printer which isn't quite up to the job of camera-ready artwork.

This machine I have such admiration for is a Xerox Docutech, residing at the Printing Department at the Western Metropolitan Institute of TAFE in Footscray. Some of the book 'makers' mentioned above use one of these. Your book is stored on disk, ready for instant reprints, it prints from A5 up to A3 and each page is registered exactly the same so that page numbers, for example, don't move around. It takes 80gsm to 200gsm stock, can enlarge, stretch, reduce and crop photos after scanning, and last-minute proofing and correction is easy. At the moment it only prints in black but a colour version should be out by the year 2000. And best of all, it's reasonably cheap.

Obviously it has limitations, such as colour work, and it can't score covers for easier folding, and odd-sized books may be a problem, but if you know of a printer who's got one, check it out.

What can you do?

If you want more than 200 copies, you should probably look at using a commercial printer of some kind, unless you've got the time and energy to put your books together yourself.

One of the best options currently is to get your covers printed — and get the best you can afford. Then find the cheapest way to get the insides printed, either by photocopying or Docutech, and physically assemble the book yourself. See Appendix 1 for hand-binding ideas. If your book will be A5 and your pages will be printed on A4, I recommend you pay to have them folded as well. Folding is the most time-consuming work of all.

If you are planning a very small print run, you can do everything yourself, even print every page out on a laser printer. A software program such as PageMaker will put the pages in the right order for you, which is a big help if you are interleaving and saddle stitching.

If you have special requirements for your book, this may dictate to some extent how and where it is printed. While you could take your photocopied book to a quick printer to be spiral

Methods of printing

bound, he would probably charge you quite a bit more for that single service than if it were included with a photocopying job, so check your quotes and do your sums. Ask around for anyone who has a comb binder which they could lend you, and buy comb bindings from a stationery supplier. They usually come in packets or boxes of 25 to 100.

What can't you do?

There are some jobs which, despite our best efforts, it just isn't possible to do ourselves and get the quality we want. One of these is trimming. An office guillotine or a ruler and cutting knife won't give you that neat professional finish to your books. If you are photocopying and binding by hand, you will already be using cut paper so it's not a problem. However, for larger saddle stitched books, where the pages creep out on the right hand side, a trim on an industrial guillotine can make all the difference. A friendly commercial printer may do this for you for a small charge, or a paper supply company could oblige.

While you can perfect bind by hand, you will probably find burst binding beyond your capabilities, due to the necessity to notch the pages. You will probably also find that books of more than 80 to 100 pages will have to be perfect bound by machine, but experiment first, especially with a hot glue gun which provides a much stronger bonding agent.

The most complicated process in any book is colour separations. It is also the most costly and for many self-publishers is not an option. Ordinary colour separations (sometimes called spot separations), where there are just two, three or four colours used in blocks can be managed with the aid of a light table. Full-colour, or process, separations, where colours are overlaid, as in photographs and reproductions of paintings, require the use of special equipment and film.

It's best to get your commercial printer to organise this work as part of the production process. Even if you fully understand how full-colour separations work and where to go for the service, you still have to facilitate two jobs instead of one and any mistakes in between will cost you dearly.

Successful Self-Publishing

Figure 12.1 Quote for printing

Book Title:
Trimmed size of book:
Number of pages:
Binding required: *Saddle stitched, perfect, burst, hard cover?*
No. of copies: *(Ask for prices on a range of print runs.)*
Paper stock: *If not ordinary bond, you will have to look at samples first.*
Text ink:
Cover stock: *Look at samples first.*
Cover ink/s: *Look at Pantone colour swatches first for exact shades.*
Artwork (pages): *How will this be supplied? Are paste-ups necessary?*
Artwork (cover): *How will this be supplied? Is any work by printer required, such as separations?*
Text proof required:
Cover proof required: *(Ask for the cost of the cover separate from the whole book.)*
Extra covers: *How many extra covers do you want?*
Freight costs: *You may need your books shipped to you.*
Required by: *Give a date 3 to 4 weeks before the launch and stick to it.*
Please quote without sales tax. I would appreciate any advice concerning improvement of quality or reduction of costs.
Your name, address and phone/fax number.
This can also be used as your initial specifications sheet.

Bromiding, or screening, is also a process which you are better off getting the experts to carry out. There is a kind of 'screen' available which is supposed to work on your black and white photographs via a photocopier, but I and several of my students have had no success with it at all.

Trying to choose your printing option can send you around and around in ever decreasing circles, even more so if you are trying to get a variety of quotes at the same time. Draw up a specification list, detailing what you want (e.g. up to three colours on cover, X or Y stock, perfect binding, photocopied insides, etc.) (See Fig. 12.1). If you know what you need to create your book, you can decide which services to get quotes on and which jobs you intend to complete yourself.

13 Getting quotes

For any printing process you should get quotes and compare prices and quality, even if only to look at the difference between printing everything on your printer at home and getting it photocopied. Some laser printers cost up to eight cents for a single-sided page.

Start by making up your own specifications sheet, if you haven't done so already (see Fig 12.1). Make sure you understand the terminology and the basics of the printing process you have selected, otherwise it will be like taking your car to the auto shop and wrestling with fuel injection and transmission fluid when all you need to know is if they're charging a reasonable price. Read some of the books available which clearly explain the different printing processes and give examples.

You may be able to tour a printing business and see first-hand how it's all done. The Book Printer in Maryborough, Victoria, offers regular tours and a newsletter. Other printers in other areas and states may occasionally do the same. Ask around — even a small printer with an offset is well worth a visit.

With a commercial printer, don't try to get quotes over the phone. It's too hard to explain exactly what you want, and it's also difficult to discover if this is a person who will be friendly, co-operative and helpful. A printer who isn't interested in the fact that this is your life's work, and treats you like the local plumber who wants business cards, is probably not going to take the time to make sure you get what you've dreamed about. On the other hand, a printer who takes an interest in your book and provides helpful advice is a treasure. The cheapest quote is not always the best.

You also need to make sure the printer is experienced with actual books. Some do mainly business work such as invoice pads, business cards and restaurant menus, and may find a perfect bound book a little out of their range of expertise. I have found the best kind of printer to be the one who delights in problem solving, and is prepared to experiment a little. One such printer I have worked with had never heard of laminating over a mounted photo on a cover, but he was happy to organise a trial run with his laminator which proved successful, saving us around $500 and the hassles of a full-colour reproduction.

Get straight answers to your questions and get your quotes on paper. A commercial printer will want to know:

- your specifications, for which you can provide your sheet (Fig 12.1)
- what you want your book to look like (show him a sample if possible)
- if anything needs to be jobbed out
- any special or fiddly jobs
- the date by which you require your books (it sounds cynical, but I always tell my students to lie about this and stick to it. If you insist to the printer that you must have your books by the last day of March because your launch is 3 April, you may get your books by 3 April. Don't admit your real launch date, which should be 3 to 4 weeks later.)

You will need to know:

- that the printer can produce your books the way you want them
- that the printer can produce them to the quality you require
- if there is *anything* which will be costly or troublesome
- the price for a range of print runs e.g. 200, 300 and 400 copies (or 1000, 1200, 1500)

Getting quotes

- the cost of your cover, separate from the overall cost of the book
- how much you will be charged, and how long you have to pay (ask for 30 days minimum).

Once you have decided on which printer to use and established a good working relationship with him, let him get on with the job. Don't hound him every few days — set a deadline by which you expect notification that proofs are ready and only call if he misses that deadline. If you have particular queries, try to get the answers you require early on.

Quick printers are more likely to do a phone quote as long as your job is relatively simple, i.e. straight photocopying. Once you have decided which quote to accept, visit the establishment concerned and get it in writing. Anything more involved, especially with a cover or binding, needs the person-to-person approach from the beginning.

With book 'makers' it definitely pays to visit, check out other publications they have done and make sure all aspects of your quote are covered. It is also an opportunity for you to see what equipment they use and how the books are made — a learning experience.

If your photocopying needs amount to only a couple of hundred copies, try avenues such as your local community centre or neighbourhood house. They may be amenable to a cheaper rate, especially if you bring your own paper, but don't encroach on their generosity too much.

What will a quote cover?

A commercial printer's quote will cover plates, paper and card stock, ink, setting up time and runs through the machine. It will also cover collating, folding, binding and trimming, plus any extras you may ask for such as separations and particular artwork. As I mentioned before, the plates and machine setup are the major cost, so unless you have ordered very expensive stock, an extra 100 or 200 copies for what seems a minimal amount will be very tempting. Remember — if the books end up sitting in boxes, you haven't published successfully, so don't get carried away!

The printer will show you a myriad of paper and card samples, so it's a good idea to know what you want before you start. Some people love the flecked, recycled papers, some want pristine white. For your cover stock, make sure it will wear well and not pick up dirt and fingermarks easily. Most commercially published books are laminated but this may be too costly for you. However there are plenty of glossy card stocks available.

Your main concern will be your cover, choosing the stock and making sure you provide artwork to the printer from which plates can be made with no further work needed (known as camera ready). You don't want to be paying your printer to move things around or do fiddly separation work, especially if you said you'd take care of it. If you have paid for a cover designer, that person should present their cover art in a form which can be printed from without further work, either on a disk or with separations already prepared. If you are preparing the cover yourself, ask the printer how he wants it. He may be able to show you samples from which you can work.

The printer may also ask for your text on disk rather than as hard copy. You need to check that your computer programs are compatible, and that everything on your disk is there, from title page to index. If the printer is working from your disk, provision of galley proofs to check nothing has been lost or changed are an absolute must. You will need to allow time for proofing and correcting galleys. It's a good idea to provide a hard copy with the disk so the printer can check for himself first. You should also be able to see a proof of your cover, at which time you can check that the colours and register are exactly the way you want them. For example, if you ask for bright colours, you don't want to end up with pastels, or vice versa. You also don't want photographs of people with orange or yellow faces.

The printer may also offer you extras or run-ons. They often do extras to allow for any mistakes such as smudged ink or binding mishaps. Some printers give you these for nothing, some at a reduced price. You may also want to consider getting extra covers printed, especially if these were expensive. If you don't

Getting quotes

need to reprint more insides, the covers can be used for publicity purposes. I have also seen people use a section of the front cover as invitations to the launch, or as publicity postcards.

With a book 'maker', your quote could cover taking your handwritten manuscript and presenting you with X number of books a few weeks later. If this is the case it will be quite expensive, as you are paying them to do everything. As with a commercial printer, you could give them a disk or hard copy and choose what kind of book you wanted, but you should compare their quote with several commercial printers before making any decisions.

A quick printer will only quote for the exact services you request, e.g. photocopying and folding. Again, compare prices and don't just stick with the nearest quick printer for convenience. Find out if anyone you have access to is using a Docutech, or even approach a few commercial printers for quotes if you're looking at several hundred copies. Be flexible and do your homework.

After getting your quotes and working out your unit cost (see Chapter 14), you may need to revise your specifications. A co-operative printer will help you with this. You should make these alterations now as it will be much more expensive later on. The further down the printing road you are, the more money it will cost you to change your mind.

My final advice is: wherever you go for quotes, take along examples of the kind of book you have in mind, especially if it has something you particularly want, such as a dustjacket or a fold-out centre page. It makes the whole process much easier if both you and the printer know exactly what you are talking about. Don't let anyone persuade you into something different, simply because they don't have the equipment to provide what you want. The time for reconsideration is after all the quotes are in.

14 Costing your book

The assumption that every self-publisher should be competing in the open market and relying on bookshops for sales is what gets many people into financial difficulties. When you consider that 40 per cent of your cover price goes to the bookshop (or 60 per cent to the distributor if you're using one), it can be pretty difficult to come out ahead, even if you sell all of your copies. You can be forced into bigger print runs in order to bring your unit cost down, but if your books don't sell (for example, if your publicity campaign misfires), then you're in trouble.

The unit cost of your book is calculated on your total printing and production costs divided by the number of copies, e.g. $2000 divided by 500 = $4.00 per copy. Commercial publishers know that big print runs keep the unit cost low, but they have sales reps and marketing departments working to sell as many copies as possible. Even so, they would consider 85 per cent of the print run sold as a good return. Now that you're getting down to the nitty-gritty of costing your book and analysing the marketplace, what will your figures reveal?

As well as the actual printing costs, there are some other points to consider:

- Are you planning to pay yourself for your work (such as typesetting) or will any profit be your payment? As self-publishers generally consider their profit is payment for their

Costing your book

efforts, it's another reason why you should try to come out ahead.
- What other money will you outlay apart from printing? Include the cost of your computer disks and paper, proofreaders, editor and specialised extras.
- In your costing, allow for copies which get damaged or lost, and those free copies used for reviews, publicity and special gifts.
- Are you planning to sell the majority of your books through a distributor and/or bookshops? This is a big question. If your print run will be in the thousands, you will need a distributor, otherwise you'll have to spend all of your time and money on visiting all those bookshops yourself. Given that distributors take 60 per cent of the cover price (of which the shops get 40 per cent), if your book is selling for $15.00 you will receive only a maximum return of $6.00 per copy. If it costs you that to print it, you're already in a no-win situation.

This is why many people fall into the trap of printing hundreds more copies to bring their unit cost down and then get stuck with books they can't sell. When you are competing in that open market, you also have to compete in terms of publicity and marketing. There's no point in your book being in a shop if no-one knows about it so you have to outlay dollars on publicising it. Does this sound a bit like a vicious circle? It is.

I spoke to one self-publisher recently who wrote a crime/thriller novel and printed 5000 copies, used a distributor and did very well. But his main aim was to get noticed so that his next book would be picked up by a commercial publisher. He succeeded in this aim, although he didn't make money on his self-publishing venture, but that didn't matter. On the other hand, I have seen an interview with a writer of horror novels who took the same gamble and lost his house.

Remember your estimates in Chapter 3? If you decided then that your first print run was going to be 300, then you can probably bypass the market place and sell all of the copies yourself. So all of your retail price comes directly to you. Here are two examples of costing — a small and a larger print run (printing costs are approximate).

Successful Self-Publishing

Book 1: a small collection of poetry, 72pp, 200 copies, mostly self-marketed and distributed apart from a few in local bookshops. Retail price $12.00.

Costs:	Typesetting, design etc by author	$0
	Printing	$1,200.00
	(= unit cost $6.00)	
Other costs:	Damaged/lost/free — 20 copies	$ 120.00
	Total Costs	**$1,320.00**

Bookshop discount (40%) on 30 copies	$144.00
Author sales income on 150 copies @$12.00	$1,800.00
Bookshop sales income on 30 copies	$ 216.00
Less costs	$1,320.00
Total profit possible	**$ 696.00**

Book 2: a novel, 200pp, 1200 copies, most sales by author. Retail price $15.00.

Costs:	Typesetting, design etc	$ 800.00
	Printing	$6,000.00
	(= unit cost $5.66)	
Other costs:	Damaged/lost/free — 40 copies	$ 226.40
	Total Costs	**$ 7,026.40**

Bookshop (40%) on 200 copies	$1,200.00
Author sales 960 copies @ $15.00	$14,400.00
Your % of bookshop sales income on 200 copies	$1,800.00
Less costs	$7,026.40
Total profit possible	**$9,173.60**

Neither of these examples allows for professional editing or publicity costs (highly recommended when you're risking thousands of dollars). It's also assuming that as the author you are going to make sure you sell *all* of your copies.

The following examples show the differences when you start talking in thousands of copies and using a commercial distributor.

Costing your book

Book 3: a mainstream genre novel, 280pp, 4000 copies, commercially distributed. Retail price $15.00.

Costs:	Editing	$1,000.00
	Typesetting, design etc	$ 1,200.00
	Printing	$10,000.00
	(= unit cost $3.05)	
Other costs:	Damaged/lost/free — 100 copies	$ 305.00
	Publicity	$ 1,000.00
	Total costs	**$13,505.00**

Distributor's discount (60%) on 3,900 copies	$35,100.00
Your 40% of distributor sales income on 3,900 copies	$23,400.00
Less costs	$13,505.00
Total profit possible *if all copies sold*	**$9,895.00**

But all copies sold is rare. Look at the same costing with 50% sales.

Book 4: a mainstream genre novel, 280pp, 4000 copies, commercially distributed. Retail price $15.00

Costs:	Editing	$ 1,000.00
	Typesetting, design etc	$ 1,200.00
	Printing	$10,000.00
	(= unit cost $3.05)	
Other costs:	Damaged/lost/free — 100 copies	$305.00
	Publicity	$ 1,000.00
	Total costs	**$13,505.00**

Distributor's discount (60%) on 1,950 copies (the rest returned to you)	$17,550.00
Your 40% of distributor sales income on 1,950 copies	$11,700.00
Less costs	$13,505.00
Total loss on 50% sales	**−$1,805.00**

Hard to believe, isn't it? And if our author only sold 1000 copies . . . I'll let you work that one out.

Some other points you may like to consider:

- Poetry suits short print runs and author sales because of your ability to sell at venues such as poetry readings, whereas distributors and bookshops often don't like handling poetry.
- Fiction can be approached like poetry — you don't have to get fixated on the 'rich and famous' syndrome. Besides, if you were honest, if you had a best-seller on your hands, don't you think a publisher would have realised that by now? Yes, there are books that were self-published that took off, but they are the exception. If word gets around about your book so that a commercial publisher picks it up, it'll just as likely happen with 300 copies as 3000 — and you won't have already encroached on their markets. Specialist non-fiction is a little different — a publisher may decide you have already covered most of the interested market. Maybe you have — and you've made the profit!
- A good publicist is worth the money, especially when you're prepared to get out and do the interview circuit. You're paying for their contacts and ability to get your book into places you can't. Ask around for recommendations as many publicists aren't familiar with books. A professional publicist will probably charge around $1000 minimum, depending on how much you want them to do.
- If you are thinking of using a distributor, contact four or five (through recommendations or the Yellow Pages under 'Book Wholesalers' or through the directory of Book Publishers and Distributors of Aotearoa New Zealand — available from the Book Publishers Association of New Zealand, phone: (09) 480 2711) and ask about their requirements. Most of the larger distributors I surveyed said they wouldn't take less than 2000 copies, and were only interested in books which competed in production quality with others on the shelves. A small distributor may take less books but they often don't have the range of outlets available. You need to be very sure of what is expected of your book and what services you will be getting.

Costing your book

- If you believe that your book will sell well but you decide to start with a smaller print run, make provision with your printer for very fast reprints and have extra covers printed in the first run. Monitor publicity, marketing and orders, set up an efficient ordering and invoicing system.
- Be businesslike about this whole process. If you are selling, approach it professionally and believe in what you are doing. Don't apologise for being a self-publisher, and don't underprice your book. You are devaluing it and so will your customers. When you've costed everything out, you may decide the market could bear you adding a dollar to your price, especially if you're offering something different. Or you could add a bookmark (or some other incentive which will be very cheap and easy for you to produce) which will temper the slightly higher price you are asking.
- If you have planned, costed and adjusted, you will be successful — you will sell 90 to 100 per cent of your copies and you will make a profit.

I have seen three different recommendations for the maximum unit cost as a percentage of your recommended retail price — 20%, 25% and 33%. If you are tackling the open market then a unit cost of 20% of RRP is recommended. If you are selling your books yourself, you can afford to go up to 33% unit cost, but try not to exceed this as you will end up out of pocket.

If you are still battling to keep your unit cost down, look at ways of reducing it. Go back to your production methods — cut a colour out of your cover, reduce the number of pages, take out some of those photos, use a cheaper paper, use a different cover stock so you don't have to laminate, etc. On small print runs you can be even more drastic, e.g. bind your book by hand instead of paying $1.00 per copy to perfect bind on a machine. Take the time to economise and hone your methods down to achieve what you want without breaking the bank. (See earlier chapters for more ideas on cutting costs.)

Now, in order to work out your unit cost, your equation will consist of:

Costs: Production, typesetting, proofing, etc $
           Editing (if relevant) $
           Publicity (if relevant) $
           Printing $

Divide your total costs by your print run to give you the unit cost.

Deduct an estimate of free/damaged copies x unit cost.

If you will be using a distributor or selling through bookshops, you will have to follow the examples given to work out your *possible* profit margin. In particular, look at your unit cost compared to what you will receive after the distributor takes 60 per cent or the bookshop takes 40 per cent.

If all of this sounds depressing, consider the American poet, Susan Polis Schutz. When she began self-publishing her poetry, she decided to go on the road to sell her books. She travelled all over the USA, probably sleeping in her car or in cheap accommodation, but she kept travelling and publishing. Eventually she set up her own company, Blue Mountain Press, and to date has sold 10,000,000 copies of her various poetry titles. Rod McKuen also started by self-publishing his poetry. The key for both of these writer/publishers was their commitment of time and energy to marketing and distribution. You may not have a million-seller in mind, but you can reach your audience if you make that investment too.

15 Preparation and printing

When you are getting close to printing, it can be very useful to create a mock-up (or dummy) of your book, using photocopies and collating and pasting everything together. Use copies of your typeset pages and photocopies of your illustrations where necessary. The mock-up helps to sort out all kinds of problems and allows for finetuning. You will be able to see if page after page of that design you thought was so nifty still looks effective or is actually downright annoying and cluttered. Points to check are:

- Do your illustrations really add to the book or are there too many? Or not enough? Are they in the right places, are they the right size?
- Are your headings effective and easy to read, are they too big and fancy or too small?
- Are there big gaps which don't look right or waste space?
- Have you allowed enough preliminary pages to fit everything in, or have you ended up with blank pages where you didn't expect them?
- Is your page numbering correct?
- Have you left good margins, particularly for your binding?
- If your book is a poetry collection, have you broken longer poems between pages in the best place? Are longer poems on facing pages where possible?

If you haven't done your index yet, now that your pages are

numbered correctly as they will be printed, you can complete this job. You can also use your mock-up to facilitate communication with your printer and to indicate more clearly how you want your book to look.

If you are providing hard copy to your commercial printer to paste up for plates, it must be clean and black. A minimum of 600dpi from a laser printer is recommended. One commercial printer I have used is fond of saying, 'You give me crap, you get crap back'. They can't work miracles on poor material. If you are pasting up your artwork, you will need to understand the printing process (eight up, etc.) and paste your pages in the right order for final folding and trimming. Artwork for the cover must be exact and ready for platemaking, i.e. separations should line up (register), titles and text should be placed correctly. If you are using a designer or having separations and film prepared, you must co-ordinate this with your printer to ensure no hold-ups. Talk to the people you are working with and make sure everyone understands what is expected, what the deadlines are, and so on.

If you are using a quick printer or organising your own photocopying, you may still need to paste up your pages, especially if you are making an A5-size book and photocopying onto A4. Your mock-up will be very handy here, as interleaved pages aren't pasted up the way they read. For example, in a 40-page book your first paste up for copying will be pages 1 and 2 and, on the reverse, 39 and 40 (see Fig 15.1 on page 104). If you have pasted on illustrations and the edges of the paper show up as lines on your photocopies, use a whiting-out agent to camouflage this. Make sure the quick printer will be using your masters, not a second-generation copy.

If your commercial printer will be printing from your disk, ensure everything is on it which will be in the book, and that it is the way you want it. Print out an entire hard copy from the disk — that way you can check it's all there and you can give that hard copy (and your mock-up) to the printer to double-check nothing has gone wrong in the transference at his end. This copy, together with your mock-up, should ensure there are no major mistakes, such as pages out of order or illustrations and photos in the wrong place.

Preparation and printing

If your printer is providing galley proofs, make sure they are ready by the day you have stipulated. Check them very carefully and don't make lots of editing changes at this point — it's your final opportunity to weed out mistakes, such as illustrations with wrong captions, not start rewriting. You will hold everything up and your costs will rise. Commercial publishers charge their authors for alterations of more than ten per cent of the text.

Things to check on your galleys include:

- The text — that everything is the way you prepared it. You should compare the galleys with your own printout and treat it like a final proofreading (so get help again). Look for gaps, misaligned headings, spelling and grammar mistakes, correct layout (margins), page numbering, sentences or paragraphs out of order. Check that all your previous corrections have been done. Lastly, check contents and index for correct page numbers.

  If you find a lot of errors, consider the possibility that either you gave the printer the wrong version of your disk and/or file, or the printer's computer has transferred the file/s incorrectly.
- The illustrations — check bromided photos for quality of reproduction, check captions, placements, sizing and order. With colour illustrations or photos, check colours are correct, registers are exact, reproduction is sharp and clear.
- The cover — check colours and reproduction quality, positioning of any text, and especially check the spelling of the title, author and blurb material and check the spine print is clear and large enough to read on the shelf.

When you get the books from your printer in their neat boxes, look at several copies from each box and check for the following:

- pages are in the right order, right way up and aligned correctly
- the binding is strong and will hold under reasonable use
- folding is neat and straight
- the covers are properly finished, clean and exactly as you proofed

Successful Self-Publishing

Figure 15.1 Pasting up a 16-page interleaved book

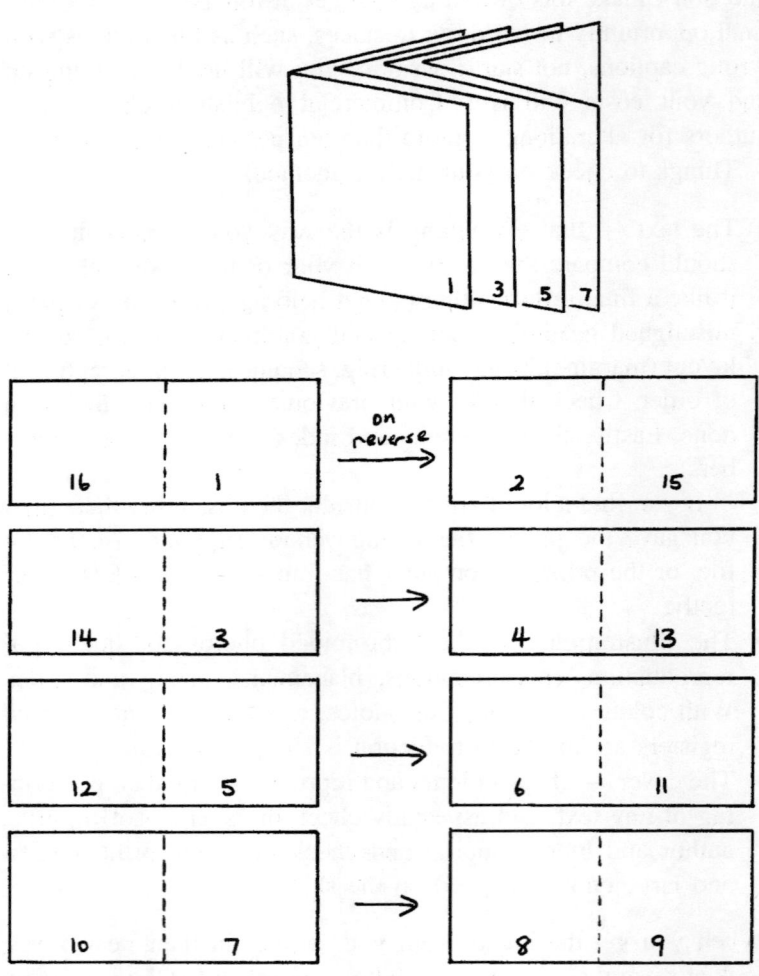

- trimming has been done properly so that margins are preserved and the trim is clean and straight with no rough edges
- also make sure the books haven't been packed while the ink is still wet — look at some of the books from the bottom of the boxes.

Preparation and printing

In other words, look for anything which makes your books less saleable. If a few books are not up to standard, don't make a fuss until you have counted how many you received, as you may have been given extras to cover these.

If the worst comes to the worst and there is a disaster, such as pages are printed out of order (usually because of a paste-up error), the computer disk is faulty or your paper stock doesn't arrive, if you have stuck to your timeline and deadlines there will be time for it to be fixed. It tends to be a case of Murphy's Law, that the tighter you have scheduled things, the more likely it is that something will go wrong. If you have given your printer a delivery date several weeks earlier than the launch date, this will also help, but don't be complacent. Keep in contact with your printer and push firmly but politely for your deadline.

If mistakes can be fixed but you're running out of time, change your launch date. You absolutely cannot afford to have a launch and publicity campaign with no books. That's the bottom line.

Finally, don't pay your bill until you have received satisfaction. You have the greatest chance of receiving what you asked for before you hand over your money.

16 Pre-publicity and the launch

You should have begun your publicity weeks or months ago, when you first started work on producing your book, simply by talking about it to friends and family and sparking interest (without boring them to tears). Along the way you should also have been gathering names and addresses of interested people to invite to the launch or, at the very least, to send some information and an order form. This is a bit different from venturing into full-on mail order as a selling option (see Chapter 17) — this is about widening your potential circle of sales as much as possible simply by making the most of interest shown. Weeks later, when you are wrestling with printing and trying to find a good launch venue, you will find it nearly impossible to sit down and recall all of those people, let alone how to contact them. For more information on advance sales, see Chapter 7.

The launch

Commercial publishers often don't think launches are worth the expense, but self-publishers should approach them as an optimum opportunity for sales. The more people you have at your launch, the more books you will sell. Those who attend, do so expecting to buy a book. So work on the principle of inviting everyone who has ever shown even the remotest interest in what you are writing, calling on friends and relatives from far and wide to

Pre-publicity and the launch

support you, and looking even further afield to clubs, organisations and societies whose members may be interested in your book. Spend some time compiling your invitation list, but don't be surprised by who does or doesn't turn up.

Find a venue that will fit large numbers of people. Don't try and skimp and have it in your backyard. Suddenly the launch becomes less official and more like just another party at your place, so people won't take it seriously (and won't buy books). If you are short of money, investigate venues such as your local library or scout hall or neighbourhood house. The local gardens may be a possibility, especially if yours is a gardening or environmental book. Look for launch venues that complement your book's subject matter.

Choose a launch date which will give you at least four weeks to get invitations out and receive RSVPs. If you don't ask everyone to let you know if they are coming, you will have to guess with your catering. Allow for those who just turn up anyway. Include information and order forms with your invitations if you like, or keep track of who doesn't attend and send them afterwards. Don't forget the old adage about 70 per cent of all books being sold in the 3 months before Christmas. It's true, so your launch could be a great opportunity for people to pick up some gifts.

You may want to advertise your launch in a newsletter such as the one published by your Writers' Centre or in *The New Zealand Author* published by the New Zealand Society of Authors, or include an open invitation in any publicity which comes out before the launch day. Not many will take up your offer, but it's worth the effort to spread the word about the book.

Ask someone to launch your book who is famous, well known or a drawcard of some kind, someone who will be interested in what you have achieved with your writing. This makes the launch more enticing for those invited as well as creating good publicity. Make sure this launcher receives a copy of your book in plenty of time to read it, ask you questions if they need to and come up with an interesting speech. As well as a copy of the book, you may want to present them with a gift on the day to say thank you.

Don't skimp on your food and drink. I have been to launches where all that was provided was cheap cask wine and some cheese and biscuits. There was a lot of muttering and not many books sold. Nice food and refreshments give the launch a sense of occasion and festivity, and add enormously to the atmosphere. You don't have to pay for catering — even if family and friends can't be prevailed upon to bring a plate, some simple sandwiches, savouries and a couple of cakes go a long way. If you can't afford bottled wine, at least decant your cask wine into carafes, or perhaps make a fruity punch. Put flowers from your garden on the table, arrange a display of materials relevant to your book (for example, old photos and mementos for a family history, a special cake from the cookbook cut by the launcher like a birthday cake, etc.). Every little extra touch will be appreciated by your guests.

Get to your launch venue early to set up. Once the first people arrive, you won't have a chance to do another thing. You shouldn't anyway — you should be concentrating on talking to guests and selling and signing books. Ask others to help out at the launch with setting out food, boiling the kettle, selling books, keeping an eye on things generally (even the occasional light-fingered guest!) Once the event gets under way, you will be the centre of attention and you will be your own best sales person, so make the most of it.

If your book is a collection of poetry or prose, make sure you read from it after the launch speech. You would be amazed how disappointed people are when they attend a launch and the author reads one quick poem or not at all. If your book is not suitable to read from in this way, prepare an entertaining speech of your own. Tell everyone how your book was produced — there's sure to be several writers in the audience who have been contemplating the same venture, and your mistakes, disasters and triumphs will be entertaining! Don't forget to thank everyone who has helped you — it's important that they all feel appreciated.

Have several excellent pens handy for signing, ones that work. You may want to decide beforehand how you are going to sign. Just your signature? A good wish of some kind? Or something individual for each person? Ask the spelling of people's names *before* you start writing in the book. Have the price clearly displayed with the piles of fresh, new copies, and have a money float which allows for large denomination notes. Keep the money in a large cash tin, not a mug from the kitchen or an old envelope. Ask someone good with sums to help with sales. You may also want to sell copies of your other books, if you have any. This is the time for special offers and discount prices, but don't lose the focus on your new book.

Have some of your order forms handy for those people who didn't bring enough money, or who have friends who might be interested. They will happily take away an order form but will probably never bother to follow up an address on a bit of paper.

Creating your own publicity material

As soon as you've set your launch date, your publicity machine should creak into action. Most self-publishers can't afford a professional publicist unless they are planning a large-scale publication. When you have to do it all yourself, you should take it seriously and apply your best writing skills to the project. You will already have a blurb which, if it is a terrific one you are happy with, can form the basis of your publicity material. However, you may want to start again.

The best way to begin is to write everything down that you want to say about your book, at least a page. Then try to come up with one phrase or short sentence that will be a catchy 'seller'. Don't feel like you are becoming some kind of marketing con-man — you are merely trying to convey to people the *essence* of your book.

From this base material you can sift out the best phrases and sentences to create your blurb, which can then be used for a press release, a flier and a general information sheet, but only if you edit and trim with *selling* in mind.

Pretend you are the customer. What would attract you to this book? What would make you want to know more about it? What more would you want to know?

Look at other books — their blurbs, their publicity campaigns, their presentation. Learn from what you think works. Don't let your own prejudices about advertising get in the way.

It is quite simple and cheap to create a publicity pack for yourself. This could include a sheet of biographical details and a photo, a flier about the book, an order form, photocopies of any newspaper cuttings about you or the book, photocopies of good reviews, and anything else you have produced such as bookmarks or badges. Don't waste these packs on all and sundry — save them for special use, when you are about to be interviewed by a magazine or newspaper, or on radio or TV. In this way, you catch the person's interest, give them all the background information they need to prepare with, and provide correct spelling and details for anything they write or say about you.

If you decide to have a business card printed, don't fall into the trap of 'labelling' yourself, i.e. JUNE BLOGGS — *Writer*, or JOE SMITH — *Self-Publisher*. A business card supplies your contact details and your business name, if you have one. The labels mentioned can sound pretentious. You want to look and sound professional.

You don't have to use expensive paper and folders for your publicity packs, nor do you have to use all of it every time. In many cases, the order form will be sufficient, along with an information sheet.

Your publicity campaign needs to get moving before the launch. Many newspapers are only interested in what's current. Work out where you will focus your campaign and plan what to send where and when. See Chapter 17 for more ideas and organise a timeline for yourself. You will find interest will fade fairly quickly so 'strike while the iron's hot'!

You may find there is a huge amount of unexpected interest in your book, because you happen to coincide with some major discovery or disaster, or even a small trend which suddenly becomes a fad (in the craft area for instance). Don't rush off and order another thousand copies of your book! But do contact your printer and alert him to the strong possibility of a reprint. Stay on top of your orders and be ready to move if necessary.

17 Distribution and marketing

Your launch is the easy part — a captive audience prepared to buy your book and appreciate your work. After the launch, you have to tackle the job of selling the remaining copies. Earlier on, you made a list of every likely buyer or selling avenue at your disposal. This list is now your basis for marketing and distributing your books.

Why wouldn't you use a commercial distributor? Firstly, because many are not interested in self-published books, often because the production quality isn't good enough and the books themselves aren't likely to have a large audience. Also, even if your print run is at least 2000 to 3000, you could make a loss because the distributor takes 60 per cent (see costings examples in Chapter 14). In order to make your book competitive in the market place, it has to compare in design, production quality and price — that's what a distributor looks for (they're a business — they want to make money too!).

If you are producing a book which fills all of those criteria, and you are ready to print 3000 to 5000 copies, either ask around for general distributors or look in the Yellow Pages. Check by phoning to make sure the company does what you want — many specialise only in remainders or educational books. Remember, you are entering the professional sales arena, so you should research how it all works, have your accounting system operating efficiently and know what to expect.

Even for small print runs, placing your books in bookshops is often more trouble than it is worth. This is because they will take at least 40 per cent of your cover price, will be reluctant to give your book any kind of prominence or promotion and generally will operate on a sale or return basis. Many large bookshops, such as Collins, Dymocks and Angus & Robertson, are very unwilling to deal with self-publishers at all. You will need to visit every bookshop yourself, present your case for them to place some copies on their shelves, and provide them with the necessary paperwork. You will find many bookshops, particularly the bigger chains, very reluctant to take your stock. There are exceptions to this of course, particularly with some of the independents such as Collected Works in Melbourne (Kris Hemensley is a wonderful supporter of new writers and publishers) and Gleebooks in Sydney. Those bookshops in country areas or your local suburb, where the bookshop owner may know you, are generally more approachable.

With this in mind, it is better if you explore other avenues and options. How can you get your book in front of a potential buyer? What will help to raise your sales potential?

Making buying easier

Always keep in mind that your potential customer can walk into a bookshop at any time and simply buy a book over the counter. It is up to you to make buying *your* book a hassle-free operation. Always carry a handy amount of change, for example, when out publicising at a reading or other venue. (Even allow for the person who only has a $50 note.)

Always carry a back-up supply in your car in case you experience a selling rush and run out. If you strike someone who is interested but doesn't have any money on them, offer them an order form and, if you think they are a genuine buyer, perhaps even give them a stamped envelope with your address already written on it.

The simpler you make it for people to buy from you, the less likely they are to walk away and forget about it.

Distribution and marketing

More publicity

After the initial flurry connected with your launch, you should follow up immediately on other methods to 'get the word around'. There are a number of ways of getting free publicity, especially at a local level. These include:

- Interviews/profiles in the local paper. Often if you approach your local newspaper they will be quite happy to interview you and print an article. Make sure you can provide a good black and white photo if their photographer is busy — they much prefer to run an article with a photo.
- Publicity after the book launch, especially if it was novel or entertaining in some way. If you found an exciting venue or had your book launched by someone newsworthy, make sure you or a friend took lots of good photos and follow up local newspapers with a couple of the best photos and a well-written account as soon as you can.
- Articles/profiles in specific magazines, e.g. if you have a gardening book, it may be possible to contribute an article to a gardening magazine and refer to your book.
- Newsletters of all kinds, from local community to business and general. Be aware of what newsletters are around in which you can request a mention, an article or even a review.
- You can try the bigger newspapers, especially if there is something different to interest them or if you have managed to get good reviews. Look at what is currently newsworthy and see if you can tap into that in some way.
- Offer to do a 'meet the writer' at the local library and help with the publicity. Advertise the fact that your book will be on sale and its price.
- Offer to be a guest speaker, perhaps at a dinner or meeting (e.g. Rotary, Apex, Lions, etc.). Again, let them know your book will be on sale and how much it is.
- Try to get interviewed on radio: community radio stations are very approachable, but even the ABC or Radio New Zealand Te Reo Irirangi o Aotearoa may be interested if you're topical or interesting in some new way. Send copies to announcers who might have a personal interest in your book or often talk

about books on their show. Anything light or funny is often suitable for breakfast shows.

Regional radio is an excellent venue for an interview and publicity. Country people listen to their radios more, especially for information and items of interest. Provide information to the station switchboard on where your book can be purchased, or your address and the price (including postage) for orders.

- Do a mail box drop in your local area with information and order forms. This is a suitable idea for local histories or books which tap into something in the area.
- Be part of a festival, especially a community festival or one with a theme that you can fit into. If you're a poet, offer a reading. If you're a gardener, have an information stall, etc.
- Try to get involved in community TV. Optus have a community channel now, and are planning a poetry show. New Zealand's main centres have community channels. Commercial TV can be a long shot, but worth having a go, particularly if you think the compere will be interested (e.g. Bert Newton in Melbourne, or New Zealand's Paul Holmes Show), or your book is on a 'hot' topic. If you do manage to get a response from a TV show, be prepared to promote yourself confidently, right from the first phone call.

Note: Handy resources for contacts in the media are Margaret Gee's *Media Guide* and Nielson Media Guide. Staff changes rapidly in this industry so use a current edition (try your library).

- You may be able to publicise your work on the Internet. Investigate how to set up a Home Page, how to organise orders.

Note: Cost this process before you rush in. If you are already connected to the Internet, contact your ISP for information and prices. There are one or two enterprises operating at the moment, aiming to promote and sell your books through their Internet site, but they're not cheap. One is currently quoting an initial fee of AUS$495, plus $95 a year, plus 10 per cent commission on sales. Compare that to how much publicity you'd get on your own for $600. New Zealand Books On Line quotes $30 per month ($360 per year) for a Level One site

Distribution and marketing

and $90 per month ($1080 per year) for a Level Two site. There are also organisations, such as the Terrapin Corporation, which will provide an independent book with its own site.
- There are plenty of readings around, try to be invited as a guest, but certainly participate in the open readings and take copies of your book to place at your elbow.
- Have good photos (preferably black and white) to offer if newspapers or other avenues require them and can't organise their own.

In all instances where your book is being mentioned, you must clearly state where people can buy the book — if it's from you, give an address or PO box number with *price including postage*. If your publicity efforts are in areas where people can't buy from you firsthand, it might be an idea to have copies of your book available in a centrally located shop for easier access. You should explain this to the bookshop owner so he or she knows that sales are more likely.

Bookshops

If you do decide to try the bookshops, keep the following in mind:

- It may be a practical idea to focus on two or three and promote them as well in your publicity — they will be receiving something extra in return.
- Find a way to get your book displayed in a prime spot in the shop, e.g. on the counter in a special box, facing outwards on the shelf, or display a colourful poster somewhere close by.
- Offer other incentives such as bookmarks to help catch the customer's eye.
- You may be able to provide a dump bin for your books — recycle one from a bookshop, they often throw them out.
- Make sure you fill out the paperwork properly, i.e. invoicing. The bigger the shop, the more likely they are to be on computer. At the very least, you want them to be able to keep minimal tabs on stock numbers for you and facilitate payment.

- If you are trying to get into lots of shops, this is where a barcode will be very useful.
- The shop will very likely take just a few copies on sale or return, often as a favour. Don't antagonise them unnecessarily — make the most of what you get.
- Look locally first and try independent bookshops next. If you have a good relationship with your local bookshop as a customer, they will be more amenable to helping you.

Reviews

Be aware that newspapers and magazines will not review your book just because you've sent it to them. Some things to keep in mind are:

- If you are sending copies out for review, include their cost in your initial budget estimates.
- Target your review copies, i.e. send them to magazines which have already published some of your work or are interested in your area.
- Don't bother about big newspapers such as *The Age*, or *Dominion*, unless you have a contact to assist you, or your publicity is likely to bring your book to their notice anyway. But do remember *Australian Book Review* and *New Zealand Books: A Review*—send them some information as well since the former publication has a 'Bulletin Board'.
- Remember that reviews often don't come out for three to six months after the book is published, therefore don't rely on them to generate sales and publicity.
- You are competing mostly with commercially published books, so you need to establish your credibility via already published pieces and the look of the book (top quality production). A small publicity package may help.

Co-operative selling

- It is always a good idea to seek out other self-publishers for co-operative ventures, even if it's only sharing a market stall. You cut your costs and have more to offer the customer.

Distribution and marketing

- Make sure that you are all in agreement about what you want to do and what is possible or feasible. How many hours people are able to sit on a stall may be a real sticking point, for example.
- Make sure that all of your books are of a similar high standard. One which is badly produced will pull down the quality presentation of the rest.
- Joining together with other self-publishers can be a benefit when approaching shops and libraries and schools. Because of the paperwork involved in each book order, these places will be more amenable to buying several books at a time instead of just one.
- You could also organise a joint book launch. Ensure you have a large venue and tell everyone who is invited which books will be available and how much they cost. This way they come prepared with extra money.

You may want to draw up a written agreement about responsibilities and how much you want to invest for outgoings, such as postage or stall costs. This is simple to do and safeguards everyone. Also you will need to agree on what you are trying to achieve, what your standards are and how you will be promoting yourselves. One writer I know, who was writing a series of fairy stories and producing them in little books, was doing very well on her own. Then two others asked to join in. One insisted on using a self-devised form of phonetic spelling (which immediately deterred parents and teachers from buying) and the other insisted on being paid $100 up front before any of her books were sold.

There is currently a support group for self-publishers meeting at the Victorian Writers' Centre. They are looking at co-operative marketing and selling methods as well as having guest speakers and sharing information and resources. If there is not one operating in your area, perhaps you could form one of your own.

Market stalls

There are dozens of weekend markets in every city, from trash and treasure to expensive craft. There is even a book out called *A Guide to Markets in Victoria* by Penny Smith (Viking). Most markets charge a stall rental fee so you need to sell quite a few copies to make it worth your while.

- Research what kind of market it is, new/craft or trash and treasure. People won't generally buy new books at a trash and treasure market.
- What kind of buying audience is it? Will they be interested in book-related products? Will they expect a cheap price?
- What is the cost of the stall? If it is over $20 you should consider sharing with someone else or getting an already established stall to stock your books. Alternatively you can stock your stall with other products.
- How can you make your stall look attractive to buyers? What will stand out, look different or imaginative? Are your displays tidy and easy to see, or browse along? Is your stall three-dimensional, looking good behind as well as in front?
- How can you attract customers to stop and look? Try readings, free samples of pages of poems, extras such as bookmarks, music playing, some kind of active centrepiece.
- Is the cover of your book attractive and 'pick-uppable'? Provide some copies with plastic over them so anyone can look and touch at leisure. These sample copies will inevitably get tatty or damaged, so use ones which might be slightly damaged already.
- Are there other writing or book-related things you can stock on your stall to cover customers' wants, e.g. bookmarks, poems written on the spot, calligraphied poems in frames, etc. (*Note:* Do not stock second-hand books — people will nearly always buy them first!)
- Have you a friend who is a busker who can perform in front of your stall (earn money of their own) and attract customers?
- Don't forget to work out the cost of running your stall. If you are working on a low-profit margin, the ongoing stall cost may be a problem, especially if sales are low. Review your progress, seasonally adjusted (don't forget that Christmas gift

period). You will find a difference between doing it only once and having a regular stall, as people will get to know you're there and look out for you.
- If your stall is a success, consider asking or paying for help to avoid impatient customers or theft.

Shopping centres

My local shopping centre always seems to have car raffles operating, but sometimes groups in the area are allowed to run stalls for fund raising. You need to approach the publicity person for the centre to make initial enquiries. Make it clear that you are an individual from the area and not a commercial business.

- Are they amenable to you as a small seller with a stall? Or do they only allow charities? Will they charge you a business rental fee? Some large shopping centres have certain weeks in the year when they allow community stalls.
- Who will your audience be (what is your book)? Is there already a bookshop there in the centre? Can you work with the bookshop in some way?
- If your book is a particular kind, e.g. a cookbook, can you work in with other kinds of shops? A cookbook may sell better in a kitchen/garden shop than a bookshop.
- Could you launch your book in one of the cafes?
- Does the shopping centre have community activities or festivals you could tap into?
- Are there shops who might be interested in sponsoring you in some way in return for advertising?

Selling through schools and community groups

In this area you can offer to put on an 'event' of some kind for the school/group which people will attend and enjoy. It's reciprocal in that you will be providing entertainment of some kind (a talk or demonstration) in return for the opportunity to sell your books. Let's look first at books which are intended for an adult audience, such as gardening or recipe books.

- Who can you make contact with (e.g. teacher or secretary) who will assist with a venue and publicity? You may need access to a stove or microwave, or a specific working area.
- What are you offering them as a fundraiser—30 per cent of your sales? Both sides need to get something out of it, and they will be more likely to help you when it's to their advantage as well.
- Your book does need to have an angle, some way to present/perform it, e.g. with a cookbook you could do a cooking demonstration. People need a reason to come along and be entertained. There are few parents' groups who will turn up for a poetry reading (sad but true!) so you should be realistic about the 'pulling power' of your book in this situation.
- You need to have a professional approach to the schools or centres, both in your offer and in your communication about arrangements.
- If you do it well, 'word of mouth' will tend to get you other venues — look further ahead than just this first time.
- Start with your local schools/groups first.
- Explore the possibility also of selling class sets to the schools.
- If the publicity isn't well planned and inviting, you won't get any customers. This is a venture which needs lots of planning, co-operation and incentives.

If your book is for children, you are still selling to parents and teachers, but in a different way. You will be entertaining the children first, so be aware that you may well get asked to do workshops or performances for the children. If it's a reciprocal deal, then you will have to set up for sales (i.e. with information and order forms sent home beforehand so children bring their money on the day).

However, many writers do school visits without necessarily working on first-hand sales as a priority. If this is the case, like any other school 'act', you get paid (most of them get up to $300 or more for a half day or day). You should ask the school if they want you to bring books along to sell as well. Even if they say no, which they are entitled to do, bring a boxful in your car, just in case.

Charity signings

If you are reasonably well known in your community, or you are a great speaker, you could contact a local charity and offer a charity signing. There would need to be an incentive for people to come along, especially if they've never heard of you before, but you and the charity people may have some ideas. For example, if your book is a recipe book, how about a bake-off competition using your recipes? The audience gets to eat the food, meet you and have their book signed when they buy one. The charity gets 40 per cent or 50 per cent of your sales. Again, both of you need to benefit.

Teachers and libraries

Approaching your nearest libraries and school librarians can be an effective way of selling a few copies because of their natural interest in local writers.

- Understand how schools and libraries usually buy their books (i.e. through reading trade publications, review magazines, etc., and ordering through library suppliers).
- Understand also how they approach buying in terms of paperwork (i.e. invoicing, orders etc.) Many libraries buy through their council finance department with requisitions and orders. This is why being able to sell them more than one title is useful (See also 'Co-operative selling').
- Focus on the possibility of class sets for schools, if not immediately then later.
- Target the right people — the acquisitions librarian perhaps, or the school librarian, as well as the appropriate teacher.
- Offer them something in return (eg a 'meet the writer' event or a reading).
- Many libraries have several branches — make sure you are approaching the main library.
- Look at the possibility of tapping into holiday programs, especially if yours is a children's book.
- Is your book appropriate for a particular program, such as

ESL or adult literacy, and can you sell a class set (along with a reading)?
- Is your book potentially useful to a tertiary institution? What courses do the TAFEs and universities in your area run? Could you be a guest speaker for a catering or horticulture course? How could you go about getting your title on a recommended reading list?

You could apply to have your book considered for curriculum use in schools. Contact the Head Office of the Department of Education in your area for more information.

Direct mail

Direct mail can be a tricky area, costing lots of money for perhaps a one per cent return. You need to think about what is involved in mail order — read some books and research the possibilities for your book. Understand the difference between blanket coverage and targeting, for example.

- Where can you get a mailing list from? It is possible to buy a mailing list of people who might be interested in your product. How much will it cost you?
- Who would you target? Why?
- How would you present yourself on paper? Can you promote yourself well?
- Can you write the advertising material required?
- Can you afford the initial cost? You would need high-quality material on glossy paper, envelopes and stamps, personalised letters if possible and probably a reply paid envelope. That could cost you more money than you could ever make in sales (that one per cent return is average).

Mail order is a viable option for self-publishers, but only if you are targeting the right people and able to effectively promote your book on paper. It is much easier to interest buyers when they are hearing you read or talk — how can you create the same effect by mail? It is worth considering a group mailout with other writers. You split the costs and provide customers with a range to choose from.

The bottom line with mail order is to know what you're doing and research the area. The success rate is much higher with how-to books because you are selling information — a very viable property. There are plenty of books around on the ins and outs of mail order or direct mail, so try your library.

On a smaller, more practical scale, consider setting up a database with writing/publishing friends, compiling names and addresses of people you already know who read books and buy them. Use contacts and friends interstate to broaden your scope.

A mail order list can also be started through initial market research surveys that you ask people to complete when you are planning your book. If you want their names and addresses, you should assure them that you won't use this information for anything other than your own book (and stick to it). Peter Brady, who wrote the biography of William Ricketts and his sanctuary in the Dandenongs, asked people who visited the sanctuary to fill out a survey. From this he could make decisions on how many photos to include, colour or black and white photos, size of the book, and hardcover or paperback. He also asked those who were interested to supply their name and address so they could be notified when the book was available. From this simple manoeuvre, he sold over 2000 copies by mail order.

Those people who order your book by mail are also the basis for future mailing lists. Keep note of all this information and build on it.

Advertising

Advertising is like mail order — you need to research who you are targeting and how to make it the most effective. Who is your buying audience and where can you best reach them? For example, children don't usually buy books, the adults around them do. No amount of advertising can persuade people to buy a book they don't need or want. Don't misrepresent your book or you'll get returns and complaints.

- How much will it cost you? The bigger the newspaper/magazine's circulation, the more it will cost.

- Research already shows that twelve small ads repeated gain a better response than one huge one.
- Can you write an effective ad to fit in a 4 cm × 4 cm space?
- Targeting is the most effective way to approach this. Look for the right place to put your ad, i.e. where readers will already be interested in what you are offering. A gardening book should be advertised in gardening magazines and newsletters.
- Dominate a small area rather than try to compete in a big one.
- Consider swapping advertising in smaller publications — your advertisement in their magazine in return for a promotional flier/order form for their magazine tucked inside your book.

Elements which may make your advertisement more effective include:

- a reply/order coupon
- a money-back guarantee
- credit card payment available
- a premium, i.e. you offer a *free* gift of some kind if they reply in fourteen days
- you could stress it's a limited offer to speed up replies so they don't forget.

Other ways of advertising may be more effective:

- cost effective 'freebies' such as bookmarks, badges, sample poems, note pads, T shirts (you wear it as your own walking advertisement) etc.
- put an order blank in the back of your book for other readers
- you are your own best advertisement, whether that is by readings, talking or how you present yourself generally — make the most of it!

Readings and talks

If your book is poetry or fiction, or something which is performable in some way, you can take advantage of the open readings which happen in all major cities and some smaller ones.

But you must remember that you are your book's best promotional tool. A poor, lacklustre reading will sell nothing. If you

Distribution and marketing

are not confident in reading or speaking, take some classes in performance or public speaking. It's a good investment, and will come in handy for interviews as well. I have seen many poets sell their books purely from the quality of their reading.

Learn how to be positive and to promote without harassing people. Nothing puts a customer off faster than having a book shoved down their throat, even if they started out interested.

If you are asked to speak at a dinner or meeting of some kind, prepare a speech properly. Very few people can speak confidently off the cuff and be entertaining as well. Rehearse!

Don't be afraid to talk about your book, how you wrote and published it, what it's about. That's part of generating interest.

Other kinds of selling venues (not bookshops)

- Approach any place where you think people may be interested in books (e.g. art galleries, craft shops, specialty shops etc.) Offer the owner the same as a bookshop — 40 per cent. He/she may be happy with less.
- Ask your friends to sell copies for you, especially if they live interstate. Offer them a free book if they sell 10. If you have a friend who is a natural sales person, offer them a percentage!
- Try places such as citizen's advice bureaus, tourist information centres, etc.
- If you offer to be a speaker at places such as Rotary or Apex, make sure those attending know beforehand who you are, that you will be selling books at what price (and make sure you entertain them).
- No matter where you leave your books to be sold, write out an invoice which clearly states the number of copies, selling agreement (percentage, sale or return, etc), recommended retail price, venue name and address, your name, address and phone number. Keep a regular check on sales and restocking.

Other ways to promote and sell

Some of these ideas may sound a bit unrealistic, but every one of them has been suggested to me by self-publishers who have found them to be workable.

- Set yourself up on a mini writer's tour, giving readings and organising your publicity and venues in advance. Melbourne poet, Peter Bakowski, has been on several tours through New South Wales and to Brisbane, with great success. He organises readings in each place he plans to visit, then also sets up radio and press interviews, timed to appear or be broadcast two or three days before his reading. He takes plenty of books and makes a point of reading well.
- Party plans — investigate if your book is appropriate to be included in a party plan for other products. If your book is a craft item (e.g. haiku on handmade paper), you could tie in with craft party plans.
- See if direct marketing groups such as Amway are interested in your book as a product.
- Investigate other kinds of distributors, e.g. there are several companies now who visit workplaces and leave books and order forms.
- Organise readings in large venues where people are already gathered, e.g. workplace canteens or cafes at lunchtime. You need to do advance publicity to let them know you will be selling books (don't organise this for the day before payday!)
- Investigate having a stall at a community trade fair (or general trade fair even). Often the cost of a stall at these fairs is expensive. You could share a stall or contribute to a larger retailer's costs. At the International Feminist Book Fair in Melbourne a couple of years ago, a dozen small publishers and magazines combined to stock and staff a stall. One stall cost over $1200, which would have been impossible for them to pay for individually.
- Look at the other places you can have a stall, such as country shows, special markets etc.

Professionals and sales people are not shy. If you shrink inside and feel ill at the thought of having to talk to strangers about your book enthusiastically, openly and inspirationally, then maybe selling is not for you. You will either have to find someone to sell for you, or accept that you may have to give your book away as a gift. There is nothing wrong in this, but when you're

Distribution and marketing

talking about print runs of hundreds of copies, selling them is going to be a very important aspect of your self-publishing venture. It's one you need to organise properly and put as much, if not more, time and energy into than the printing and production, otherwise you will have wasted your hard work and money. Remember that realistic, honest approach you started out with? Now that you've read and thought about what's required to get out there and sell your book, are your answers still the same?

Hopefully, you've read about all of these selling opportunities and they have inspired you. Work out which ones will suit you best in terms of time and energy and plan a sales strategy. When you've sold 90 per cent of your books and the mistakes you made have receded into distant memory, take time to read Chapter 18 and review your accomplishments.

18 Finally . . .

For many people there is a hectic four to six week period after the launch where they focus on publicity and selling and then the furore starts to die down. If your book is not selling, you will have to review your marketing plan, make alterations and incorporate new strategies, then continue the hard work.

If your print run was too large, your marketing will have to be extended and more avenues explored. If you are in the fortunate position of selling all of your copies in the first few weeks, you are then faced with the decision of whether to reprint or not. Have you covered all of your opportunities for sales yet? If you have, you've succeeded well and may decide to only reprint another 50 copies (easily done if you ordered those extra covers). If you still have avenues to pursue and are confident of many more sales, do another sensible estimation and then reprint.

If your book has sold well to the customers you were able to reach and you believe there is a much wider market to be tapped, this may well be the time to approach a commercial publisher.

Reviewing finances

By the six-week mark, you should have paid your printing bill and paid back any money advanced to you by friends and family. If you placed books in bookshops and other selling venues, now is the time to check sales, collect money and restock where necessary. If you leave it too long, your books and paperwork are likely to disappear.

You should ensure that any orders have been filled, and have investigated sales to local libraries and schools, if not further afield as well. All of your bookkeeping and paperwork should be up to date.

Who keeps what?

You should keep at least three copies for yourself, in mint condition. Sign and date them the day of the launch and store them safely.

If your printer is not keeping artwork for reprints, make sure you get all of it back and store it carefully where it won't get damaged or creased. Your early drafts and manuscript should also be stored away — one day they might be of value to librarians and archivists.

Remainders

If you printed far too many copies, don't despair. Give yourself two years in which to sell them. The initial rush will slow to a trickle but if you take them everywhere you go and continue a steady promotion, they will sell, albeit slowly.

After two years, you have several options:

- Pulp them, i.e. hand them over to a recycler to be made into paper and card for someone else. This can be depressing but sometimes less so than boxes of books going mouldy.
- Approach a remaindering company. These are listed in the Yellow Pages under book wholesalers (as are distributors so check to make sure you contact the right ones). Remaindering companies may not be interested — if they are, you will not receive very much money.
- Use your surplus books as 'freebies' with your next book! Known in the trade as premiums.

Evaluation time

After a few weeks or months, when you've stopped having

nightmares or wishing you'd never started the whole business, you'll be ready to evaluate your self-publishing venture.

What mistakes did you make? Why? Did you run out of time? Did you use a printer who let you down? Did you over/underestimate your print run? Did your costing work out? What succeeded? What new skills did you learn? What was the best part? What was the best moment? Did your book look the way you imagined it would? How could you have improved it?

These and many more questions are worth pondering. It is a rare self-publisher who is completely happy with everything. It seems to be in our nature to always want to improve our books as soon as they're in our hands!

So . . . when are you publishing the next one?

Appendix 1
Hand binding

To prepare your covers for hand binding, you should measure the thickness of your book by assembling the total number of pages (use blank paper of the same weight). Measure at the spine edge and add approximately 2mm for each fold, depending on the weight of your card stock. From this you can work out the size of your cover (Fig. 1.1).

[Back Cover] + fold allowance + spine + fold allowance + [Front Cover] = ?

A. A small book or magazine (A5 size) up to 40pp.

It is a good idea to use folded A4 pages, uncut. This may mean a different layout in your paste-up stage, so experiment first with a mock-up. Lay the folded pages on top of each other, not interleaved (Fig 1.2).

For extra strength, you can staple through the spine edge two to three millimetres in. After gluing, these staples won't show. Your pages are then fixed in place and won't move around when you attach the cover. You can also sew your pages together if you have a suitable sewing machine (we have used an old industrial Singer). Sew two to three millimetres in from the spine edge. Sewing will reduce the thickness of your book (it compresses the paper more) so you will need to remeasure sewed sections.

If you decide to cut your pages before gluing, use a sharp artknife or Stanley knife and a steel ruler to cut accurately. After cutting, 'knock down' your pages, i.e. tap them on the table so the top, right and bottom edges are even. If the binding edges are slightly uneven it won't matter too much.

If you use a commercial printer for your covers, you should mark score lines for him (scoring makes folding easier). If you are scoring your own covers, use a bread and butter knife (not serrated) and a steel ruler. Fold your covers on the score lines before gluing. Run a line of PVA glue or hot glue down the inside of the cover spine area. If using hot glue, you will need to move reasonably fast before it dries. PVA glue has the advantage of drying clear, especially if you accidentally use too much. With PVA, leave about 1.5cm free at the top and bottom of the spine to allow it to spread. (Fig 1.3)

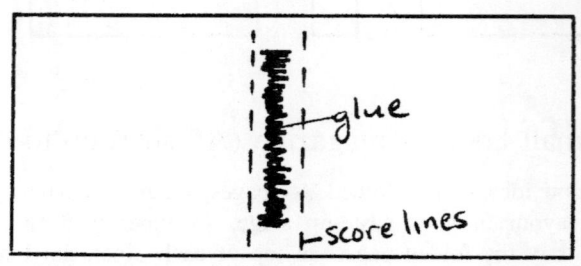

Appendix 1

Place pages into glued spine, wrap the cover around and check that it's straight. Place the finished books under a medium-weight, flat object (a large encyclopaedia is handy!) and leave for 24 hours or until dry. Weights which are too heavy will squash or bow your spines.

B. Larger books 40–100pp.

The best method for larger books is to use cut pages. Perfect binding machines roughen the edges to take more glue. If you wish to do this, stack about 10 to 15 books together and use an artknife or similar — be very careful.

Alternatively, you can apply a preliminary layer of glue to this stack with a small paintbrush and slightly diluted PVA glue. Fan the pages sideways (at about a 20 to 30 degree angle) to allow more glue to penetrate (Fig 1.4). For ease of separating later, you can place a piece of coloured paper between each book.

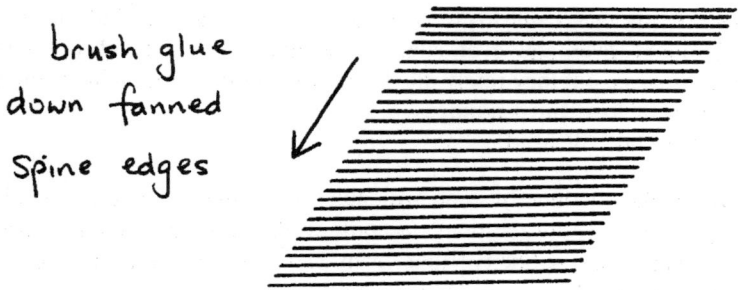

After this preliminary gluing, separate the books and knock down gently to even up. Have your covers ready, glue down the inside of the spine, place pages inside and wrap around. Make sure outside edges are square with the cover, place under heavy, flat objects to dry.

With larger books, you can sew sections together (10 to 15 leaves at a time) and then glue these sections into the cover. Remember with these larger books to measure the total thickness of the pages as accurately as possible and allow a little extra for folding.

Your book has more than 100 pages? It is still possible to bind by hand but I would certainly recommend hot glue in that case as it bonds more strongly, so long as you can work fast and accurately.

As with anything, perfect binding by hand takes practice. Buy some card and use scrap paper to make up half a dozen books until you can gauge spine and folding allowances, the amount of glue needed and how best to keep your pages straight.

Appendix 2
Starting and publishing a magazine

The main difference between self-publishing a book and starting a magazine is that a magazine is ongoing — you have to find the time and money over and over again. It would be nice if subscriptions covered costs, but they rarely do. Therefore running a magazine is often a labour of love and learning.

What you will need:

- a regular amount of time available for publicity, editorial work, typesetting — all the things a book needs but on a continual basis;
- to start your publicity right from Day One so you can receive submissions from interested writers;
- an ISSN instead of an ISBN;
- to allow free copies for all your contributors;
- a large postage budget;
- to be aware of the magazine market, that some mags are trying now to compete with books — you're better off staying small and keeping your price reasonable;
- to stick to your deadlines — when a magazine starts appearing late or irregularly, subscribers and contributors think it's about to go down the gurgler and stop their support;
- to decide what kind of magazine yours will be — poetry, short fiction, special interest, literary, whatever — and stick to that until popular demand shows a change will be advantageous. Don't try to be everything to everybody or you will end up with a mash of no real interest to anyone;
- to respect your contributors' work. You will receive lots of submis-

Starting and publishing a magazine

sions which are inappropriate or very amateurish. Everyone has to start somewhere and your magazine might be their first-ever step into trying to get published, a scary feeling;
- to make your rejection letters reasonably kind and encouraging. Most editors don't have time to write critiques for contributors, so don't feel guilty if you can't or don't want to either;
- to produce a magazine which is inexpensive but looks good, which can be done by photocopying and stapling, especially if you take care with your page design and covers. Don't scrimp so much that your magazine looks cheap and nasty or no-one will want to be published in it or buy it.

Appendix 3
Bibliography

References in the text were to the following self-published books:

Campbell, Margaret, *On the Outside, Looking in* (poetry, 1994), *Passport to Wonder* (young writers' anthology, 1997), *A Pocket Full of Fairies* (two series of six fairy stories for children, 1995, 1996).
Clark, Sherryl, 1991, *Edge* (poetry), Pariah Press.
Clark, Sherryl & Campbell, eds., 1996, *In Our Time* (oral history).
Henry, Kristin, 2nd ed. 1993, *Slices of Wry* (poetry).
Just, Malcolm, 1995, *Oh Yes, The Crunchy Bits* (poetry).
Kirwan, Sylvia, 1996, *No Time For Tears* (family history).
Neate, Lorraine, 1993, *Free Spirit* (poetry).
North, Helen, 1994, *Field Days: Recollections of a Kergunyah Childhood* (biography).
Pengilley, Patricia, 1996, *Kite With Severed String* (novel).
Rolfe, Tracey, ed., 1996, *The Gallery Poems* (poetry — limited edition).
Simpson, Neil, 1994, *Macedonia: Its Disputed History* (history).
Swinton, Adrienne Mazer, 1993, *Fierce Flash* (children's picture book).
Western Women Writers, eds. Issue 1, 1993–Issue 8, 1997, ongoing, *Poetrix* (magazine of women's poetry).

Enquiries about any of the above can be directed to PO Box 532, Altona North, Vic 3025.

General references

Australian Government Publishing Service, *Style Manual: For Authors, Editors and Printers*, 5th edn, AGPS, Canberra.
Australian Government Publishing Service and Lincoln University

Bibliography

Press, *Write Edit Print: Style Manual for Aotearoa New Zealand* 5th Aust. edn, 1st NZ edn, Lincoln University Press, Canterbury.

Books in Print, D.W. Thorpe, Port Melbourne, Victoria.

Books in Print, Lincoln University Press, Canterbury.

Bundy, Judith, ed. 1993, *Directory of Library Suppliers Used by Australian Libraries*, 3rd ed., Auslib Press, Adelaide.

The Desktop Publisher's Manual, 1994, Blueprint.

Edwards, Hazel, 1997, *Writing a 'Non-boring' Family History*, Hale & Iremonger, Sydney.

Goldberg, Natalie, 1986, *Writing Down the Bones*, Shambhala, Boston.

Golvan, Colin, 1989, *Words and Law: A Practical Guide for All Those Whose Business is Writing*, Penguin, Ringwood, Victoria.

Golvan, Colin & McDonald, Michael, 1986, *Writers and the Law*, Law Book Company, Sydney.

Laurence, Janet, *The Craft of Food and Cookery Writing*, Allison & Busby.

McColl, Peg, 1992, *The Sub-licencing Guide: A Handbook of the Most Commonly Requested Uses of Copyright Material*, for the Australian Book Publishers Association Ltd.

Mandel, Judy, *Book Editors Talk to Writers*, John Wiley & Sons.

McLean, Gavin, 1992, *Local History: A Short Guide to Researching, Writing and Publishing a Local History*, Bridget Williams Books in association with National Archives, Wellington.

Miller, Patti, 1996, *Writing Your Life: A Journey of Discovery*, Allen & Unwin, Sydney.

Murray-Smith, S. 1990, *Right Words: A Guide to English Usage in Australia*, 2nd edn, Penguin Books Australia, Ringwood, Victoria.

National Library of New Zealand, *New Zealand Library Symbols 1997*, National Library of New Zealand, Wellington.

Parsons, J., 1994, *New Zealand Writer's Handbook*, David Bateman, Auckland.

The Penguin Working Words: An Australian Guide to Modern English Usage, Penguin, Ringwood, Victoria.

Pocket Pal, Associated Pulp and Paper Mills with the permission of the International Paper Co. of USA, 2nd edn, Camberwell, Victoria.

Rogers, A., 1994, *Write and Be Published: The complete guide to publication of your book*, Reed Books, Auckland.

Rogers, Geoffrey, 1985, *Editing for Print*, Writer's Digest Books, Cincinatti, Ohio.

Ross, T. and Ross, M., 1994, *The Complete Guide to Self-Publishing*, 3rd edn., Writer's Digest Books, Cincinatti, USA.

Schwarz, Samantha, 1995, *Australian Guide to Getting Published*, Hale & Iremonger, Sydney.
Strunk, W. Jr. & White, E.B., 1979, *The Elements of Style*, 3rd edn, Macmillan, New York.
Wellisch, Hans H., 1991, *Indexing from A to Z*, H.W. Wilson Company, Bronx, New York.
Whitireia Publishing, 1993, *First Editor: Notes on Publishing*, Whitireia Publishing.
Williamson, H., 1983, *Methods of Book Design*, Yale University Press, New Haven, Connecticut.

Glossary

acknowledgement Expression of appreciation from author to those who assisted with the book.
acquisitions librarian The librarian who is responsible for buying books for the library.
advance subscription Advance sales of book before printing to help with finances.
anthology A collection of writing by different authors.
area composition Composing pages electronically, by using a software program such as Pagemaker or Quark Express, including text and illustrations. Finished pages can be used directly for reproduction.
art paper High quality paper with china clay coating, available in range of finishes from matt to gloss. Excellent reproduction standard.
artwork Text and/or illustrative material prepared for printing or reproduction.
ascender The part of the letter which rises above the *x-height*, e.g. in 'd' or 'h'.
backlist Previously published books still available from the publisher.
back margin The inside margin of a page, next to the spine.
back matter See *endmatter*.
back up Printing on the reverse side of a sheet, e.g. printing pages 2 and 39 on the reverse of pages 1 and 40.
bar code A printed code of vertical lines and numbers which identifies a product. In books, the bar code is usually printed on the

back of the cover and also represents the *ISBN*. Bar codes are read by scanners in shops and warehouses.

bibliography List of books used by the author as reference materials in the writing of the book.

binding edge The edge of a book along which it is bound, usually the left hand edge.

bleed Where an illustration or photo is printed to run off the edge of the page instead of having a margin around it.

blurb The description of the book, which is one of its main marketing tools. Usually printed on the back cover or front flap of the dust jacket.

body matter Text of a page (not including headings, etc), or the main text of a book not including front and back (end) matter.

bolts The folded edges of printed sheets which are opened by trimming or slitting.

bond paper Writing and photocopying paper, usually 80 to 90gsm, reasonably thick and strong.

border Design or frame or rule around an area of type or an illustration.

bromide A reproduction of a photo or illustrative material on photographic paper, where the material is transferred into patterns of dots to represent shading for printing purposes.

bubble jet printer See *ink jet printer*.

bullets Small black dots used for lists, etc. for clearer reading.

burst binding Where notches are cut into the spine of the book to allow better glue dispersal in the binding process before the cover is attached.

camera-ready copy/artwork Material which is fully prepared, either by electronic composition or pasteup, and ready for plate making or photocopying.

caption The explanation provided for photos and illustrative material.

casting off Estimating how many typeset pages there will be from a manuscript.

centre spread The two middle pages, especially where there is illustrative material which will be printed across them.

chapbook Small book, usually saddle stitched, produced in short print runs. Often used for poetry.

character A letter, number, symbol or punctuation mark in a font or typeface.

Glossary

clean proof A proof which is fully correct, including all previous corrections.

ClipArt Copyright free illustrations available on computer disk or in books.

coated paper See *art paper*.

collate Collecting together all the printed pages in the correct order, usually for binding.

comb binding A type of binding which punches holes in the back margin of the book and threads a plastic binding strip through.

commercial printer Printer who operates as a business, printing everything from business cards and posters to menus and books.

contents The list of chapter titles and headings in a book, with corresponding page numbers.

copy All of the text and illustrations which are to be included in the book.

creep The movement of pages on the foredge when a lot of pages are interleaved. Often happens in saddle-stitched books and requires trimming with attention to retaining margins.

cropping Trimming or masking off the parts of a photo or illustration which are not needed.

cyan The blue colour used in full (four) colour process and printing.

dedication Inscription in front of book to honour someone special to the author.

descender The part of the letter which drops below the *x-height*, e.g. in 'j' or 'y'.

desktop publishing The use of a computer and appropriate software to produce camera-ready artwork, as distinct from phototypesetting.

direct mail Selling of a book or product by direct approach to potential customers through the mail, often by personally addressed letters.

distributor Commercial operator who distributes books to bookshops, newsagents and other retail outlets for a percentage of the retail price. Also called wholesaler.

dot matrix printer A printing machine which prints characters by impacting through a ribbon, either 9 pin or 24 pin.

dots per inch (dpi) The number of dots which make up the standard of printing from a laser or bubble jet printer, the higher the number the better the quality. Also used in screens/bromides.

drilling Holes made in paper, e.g. for loose-leaf binding.

drop The distance from the top of the type area to the first actual line of text.

dummy See *mock-up*.

dump bin Cardboard display bins used by bookshops to promote new books.

dust jacket High quality wrapper around book which protects it and makes it look attractive. The actual cover underneath is often plain and unprinted.

electronic publishing Publishing by electronic means so that the material is available first on a computer screen, rather than on paper.

em A unit of measurement based on the square of a given type size, roughly equivalent to the size of the letter 'm' in that typeface.

en Half of an *em*. Roughly equivalent to the size of an 'n'.

endmatter All the material which follows the body of the book, such as glossary and appendices.

endnotes Reference notes printed at the end of a chapter or at the end of a book.

endpapers A pair of leaves pasted at the front and back of a book. They help to support the binding, but are also often decorative, as in marbled paper.

erratum A notice printed and inserted in the book after it has been published, correcting mistakes found too late to be avoided.

figure An illustration or diagram, usually numbered for reference.

fixed costs Those production costs in a book which don't change regardless of how many copies are printed. They include typesetting, editing, design and plates. See also *variable costs*.

flier A sheet, usually A4 size, which is an advertisement or information about a book easily posted or handed around.

flyleaf A blank leaf, usually at the beginning of a book.

fold-out A larger sheet, bound or fixed into a book, which is folded down to page size or less, and can be unfolded for reading.

folio 1. A page number. 2. A leaf in a book.

font A complete range of characters in a particular typeface and size. Strictly speaking, it doesn't include bold and italics.

footer Information set in the foot margin of the page, usually includes page number and often the title.

footnotes Notes which expand on information in the text, or provide

Glossary

a reference. Printed either at the bottom of the relevant page, or sometimes at the end of the chapter.

foredge The outer margin of the page.

foreword A message or short piece at the front of the book, not written by the author.

format The size and shape of a book, could also include its general appearance and aspects of production, such as binding. In desktop publishing, format is the setting up of the page — layout, placement of material, font, etc.

four-colour printing Printing using cyan, magenta, yellow and black to reproduce colour photographs, paintings, etc.

galley proofs Proofs of typeset material as it will be printed, before the sheets have been divided up into pages.

gatefold cover A cover with flaps at the *foredge* which are folded in.

glossary A list of definitions relevant to the book.

grammage See *gsm*.

gsm Grams per square metre. Method used to measure paper and card, e.g. heavy card would be 200 or 240gsm.

gutter The space between two pages on a sheet, or between two columns.

half-title Title printed in a smaller typeface on the page before the title page.

half tone A photo or illustration which has been converted into dots in the bromiding/screen process for printing.

hard copy Material printed out on paper.

hard cover A book enclosed in a card and cloth case, usually with a dust jacket, as distinct from a *paperback*.

head The margin from the top of the page to the top of the type area.

header Information set in the head margin of the page, usually includes page number and often the title.

imposition The arrangement of pages on large sheets, usually for plate making, which, when printed and folded, will be in the correct order.

imprint The identifying name of the publisher carried on the book.

index An A-Z list of subjects showing where to find material in a book.

ink-jet printer Also *bubble jet*. A printer which forms characters on the paper with a stream of tiny, electrostatically charged ink drops. Not usually waterproof.

ISBN International Standard Book Number. An individual number which identifies each book.

ISSN An individual number which identifies each serial publication or magazine. Each issue will have the same ISSN.

justify To align text and other matter to a particular vertical margin or measure. Most books have text justified on both the left and right.

kerning Reducing the space between letters.

laminating A process which applies a thin layer of plastic to covers for protection and appearance.

landscape A page which is wider than it is deep.

laser printer A printer which creates characters on the paper by burning the image with a small laser.

leading The amount of white space between lines of text.

leaf The front and back of a single sheet of paper, i.e. two pages.

lower case Small letters, as distinct from capital letters.

magenta The red colour used in four-colour printing.

make-up Arranging text and illustrations into pages.

manuscript The author's typed or handwritten copy of their book. Abbreviation is ms.

margins The white space surrounding the type area on a page.

masking Isolating parts of an illustration or photo for reproduction. Masking is also used for isolating colours.

master Original camera-ready artwork.

matt finish A dull finish on card or paper.

mock-up A model of what the book should look like when finished. Can be detailed or sketched in.

orphan The first line of a new paragraph which is on its own at the bottom of a page. See also *widow*.

overlay Separate part of an illustration on transparent paper. When all the overlays are placed on top of each other, the entire illustration is present. Often used as *camera-ready artwork*, with *PMS* colours stipulated.

overs Extra copies of a book printed above the number requested.

page proof A proof of the page after it has been made up.

pagination The numbering of pages in a book.

paperback A book bound in a soft cover, usually by perfect or burst binding.

Glossary

paste-up Fixing camera-ready artwork on large sheets ready for plate-making or reproduction.

permission Authorisation from copyright owner for use of work.

perfect binding A binding where the edge is trimmed and roughened to take the glue, then placed into a soft cover.

phototypesetting A typesetting process which uses computer equipment, laser technology and a photographic process to produce material on bromide paper. Provides a very high quality of artwork but is expensive.

pica A measure in printing which equals 12 *points*.

plate Used for printing, usually on offset or web presses. Metal plates don't stretch and can be re-used. Paper plates are cheaper and used only once, but can still print thousands of copies.

PMS Pantone Matching System. International system for specifying exact colours for designers and printers.

point The basic unit for measuring type and spacing. It is equal to approximately 0.35mm.

portrait A page which is taller or deeper than it is wide.

p. or pp. The abbreviations for 'page' and 'pages'.

preface The introduction to a book written by the author.

preliminary pages All those pages which come before the body of the text. Can include contents, preface, acknowledgements, etc. Often referred to as front matter.

premium A book which is given away free as part of a publicity campaign.

pre-press All of the tasks which must be completed before plates are put on the press for printing.

process inks The standard colour inks for four-colour printing.

proof Any print-out or reproduction made in order to check for errors.

pseudonym A pen-name used by the author to conceal their real name.

public domain Any work which may be freely used is in the 'public domain'. The copyright may have expired or is not applicable.

publicist The person who is hired to promote the book through a publicity campaign, with press releases, media appearances and interviews.

ream A quantity of paper, usually 500 sheets. Most photocopy paper is sold in reams.

recto The right-hand page of a book, the odd numbered page.

register The exact alignment of separations in printing, either colours or text.

register marks Crosses or lines on artwork which act as guides to achieve register.

remainders Copies of a book sold at greatly reduced prices, to clear them out of stock.

reprint A further printing of a book with no corrections or rewriting. A new edition usually has substantial changes.

returns Books which have not been sold and are returned to the publisher for credit or refund.

review Critical analysis or discussion of a book, usually published in newspapers and magazines.

rough An artist's preliminary sketch or layout for client.

run The number of copies to be printed.

saddle stitching The binding process most commonly known as stapling through the centre fold.

sale or return Only terms on which many bookshops will take books in small amounts from self-publishers. No money is exchanged until books are sold, what is unsold is returned.

sans serif Typefaces without serifs, as in Helvetica or Arial.

scanner A device which transfers material into digital material which can be saved into computer memory.

scoring Creasing in a sheet, usually card, to make folding it easier.

screen Used to convert illustrative material into dots or lines for printing. See also *bromide*.

section A printed sheet of 4, 8, 16 or 32 pages. The number of pages on a sheet usually depends on the capacity of the printing press used.

separations Components, often colours, in artwork which are separated into *overlays* ready for plate-making.

serif Serif typefaces have small strokes on the characters, e.g. Times and New Century Schoolbook.

sheet A piece of paper which is available in a range of standard sizes.

showthrough When the paper used is too thin and printed text shows through from the other side.

side stitching Securing a book by stapling through the back margin of the pages.

sizing Increasing or decreasing the size of an illustration to fit a certain space.

Glossary

specification sheet A set of instructions which describes how the book is to be produced.

spine The binding edge of a book, where the author and title can be printed. A book with a spine is much easier to find on a shelf.

spot colour Use of colour in blocks in separations, where final colours will not be blended as in four-colour work.

standing matter Type, film and plates used to print a book which is held in case a reprint is needed.

stipple A pattern of dots which forms an area of shading or tone, i.e. in a screened photo.

stock Paper or card used in printing.

style sheets Pages of instructions or diagrams used to ensure layout of book is consistent. Also used for style and language consistency in text.

tail The margin from the bottom of the type area to the bottom of the page.

tailpiece The illustration or decoration at the end of a chapter or book.

tip-in A page which is printed separately and glued into the finished book.

trim Removal of uneven edges from a book.

trim size The finished size of the book after trimming.

typeface The complete range of all characters and styles (bold and italic) in all sizes of a type design.

type family As in typeface, but including condensed, expanded, light face and other versions.

type size The size of a typeface in points.

typesetting A general term used to cover keyboarding of copy for proofing, either on a computer, typewriter or typesetting machine.

unders The number of copies printed which are less than the number ordered.

variable costs Those costs in publishing a book which are affected by the number of copies printed, e.g. running costs of the press, ink, paper and binding. See also *fixed costs*.

verso The left-hand page of a book, the even numbered page.

webb-offset A printing press which prints from rolls of paper rather than sheets.

widow The last line of a paragraph which ends up on its own at the top of a new page.

working title A title temporarily assigned to a book until a final title is decided on.

x-height The height of a lower case 'x' in a typeface or font, (excluding the *ascender* or *descender*).

Index

acknowledgements 71–2
advance sales 17, 51; by subscription 51
advertising 123–4
anthologies 28
appendices 72
Arts Law Centre 35
Australian Copyright Council 30
Author's Fund (NZ) 37

back of title page 71
bar codes 33–4
bibliography 72
binding 54, 60–2; burst 61–2; comb or spiral 61, 87; perfect 61, 81; saddle stitch 60–61; section sewing 62; (*see also* design)
blurb 81–2
Book Bounty 17, 34
book 'makers' 66, 85, 91, 93
book shops 112, 115–16
Books in Print 33
bubble jet printers 41
burst binding 61–2
business of self-publishing 6, 23, 34

captions 75–6
card stock 59–60, 80
Cataloguing-in-Publication 33
CD-ROM 37, 38
charity signings 121
colour separations 87
columns 58
comb binding 61, 87
commercial printers 89–91
community groups, sales to 119–20
computers, use of 22–4, 40, 41–2

contents 71
co-operative selling 116–17
copyright 29–30, 31–2
Copyright Agency Limited 37–9
Copyright Council of NZ 30
Copyright Licencing Limited 39
cost cutting 50
costing examples 96–7
cover 63–5, 78–82; artwork 79; design 63–5, 81 (*see also* dust jackets)
creep 61, 87
critiquing of manuscript 25–6

dedication 71
design 53–8; book size 53–4; professional designers 63–5, 92; style sheet 56, 64; typefaces 56–8
desktop publishing 41–2, 43
diagrams 76
direct mail selling 122–3
distribution 11, 111–12
distributors 95, 98, 111
documents, use of original 76–7
dust jacket 62, 80, 82

editing 24–8
editors, freelance 26–8

fonts (*see* typefaces)
footnotes 72
foreword 71
fund raising 51–2

gatefold cover 63, 80
glossary 72

half-title page 70
hand-made books 49, 80
hard-cover books 62
how-to books 5

illustrations 73–4; copyright 31–2, 73
imposition 50
imprint page (*see* back of title page)
index 72–3
ink 60
Internet 35–6, 114–15
introduction 72
ISBN 32–3
ISSN 32–3

kerning 58

laminating 60, 80–81
laser printers 22, 41, 67–8
launch 106–09; invitation list 106, 107; venue 107
leading 58
libel 35
libraries, sales to 121–2
local histories 4

maps 76; copyright 31–2
market research 16
market stalls 117–19
marketing 14, 112–27
mock-up 101, 102

offset printing 83–4
order forms 109, 112

paintings, copyright of 31–2
Pantone Matching System 60
paper 59–60; acidity 59; size 59–60, 67; whiteness 59
partnerships 4
paste ups 102
perfect binding 61
permissions 30–31, 68; sample letter 38
photocopying 47–8

photographs 74–5; copyright 31–2; library collections 75
plagiarism 35
planning 18
preface (*see* introduction)
print run 15
production 16
proofreading 44–6, 103
public domain 31
Public Lending Right 36–7
Public Record Office 21, 72
publicist 98
publicity 109–10, 113–15

quick printers 47–8, 84–5, 91, 93
quotes 32

readings 124–5
research 21–2
reviews 116

saddle stitch (*see* binding)
saving money (*see* cost cutting)
schools, sales to 119–20, 121–2
screening (*see* bromides)
section sewing 62
shopping centres 119
spine 54, 61, 65
spiral binding 61
style guides 43–4
style sheet 44

timeline 18–20, 68–9
title page 71
titles 14–15, 24
typefaces 56–8
typesetting 42–3; phototypesetting 43
typewriter 40–2
typist 42

underwriting 51
unit cost 94, 99–100

vanity publishing 1

Xerox Docutech 48–9, 85–6